Praise for *The Top 50 Questions Kids Ask*
(Pre-K through 2nd Grade)

"If you've ever been stumped by a question your child has asked you, this book will help. Dr. Bartell identifies the 'hot-button' questions that consistently come up and actually provides the best possible answers to those questions so parents don't have to come up with them on their own on the spur of the moment."

—Elisa Ast All, cofounder, iParenting Media, and
executive editor of Disney Mom & Family Portfolio

"Finally, a book that answers all those questions we parents go in a cold sweat about! Dr. Susan tackles the tough ones such as money, shyness, siblings, and religion. Plus, we get the psychology behind it all to better understand our kids. You'll find yourself using this book every day."

—Pam Atherton, journalist and host of
A Closer Look radio talk show

"Tremendous, reassuring wisdom in an easy to access format!"

—Grace Housholder, editor of *Great Fort Wayne
(Indiana) Family* magazine

"Bill Cosby was correct—kids do say the darndest things. They also ask the darndest questions. What a stroke of brilliance to have captured these questions and then to provide parents with the best way to respond to each. Dr. Susan Bartell has once again found a way to offer sensible, succinct, and straightforward advice in yet another amazing book."

> —Sara Dimerman, Psych. Assoc., child and family therapist, author of *Character Is the Key* and *Am I a Normal Parent?*

"Dr. Susan is highly gifted at helping parents and kids connect from the heart. This book honors our innate wisdom, supports us in nurturing our kids' emotional growth, and empowers us to be the parents we were meant to be."

> —Renee Peterson Trudeau, life balance expert/coach and author of *The Mother's Guide to Self-Renewal: How to Reclaim, Rejuvenate and Re-Balance Your Life*

"If you value good sense, and you need some advice that works—in the heat of a tricky moment with your kid and long-term, too—this is the parenting guide for you."

> —Sarah Smith, editor-in-chief of *Kiwi* magazine

"*The Top 50 Questions Kids Ask* is an insightful guide on the issues and concerns every parent and child faces. It's a must-read guide that both moms and dads should keep at their bedside."

—Allison O'Connor, founder and editor
of SingleMindedWomen.com

"Dr. Susan Bartell is the go-to person for *all* questions kids ask. No one is better qualified or more in touch with this age group to lend her expertise to a book that aids parents in improving communication with their ever-curious children."

—Renee Raab Whitcombe, author of
Look Who's Going to Be a Big Sister and
Look Who's Going to Be a Big Brother

"As a mother of three, I know the many questions kids ask and how often parents can be caught off guard. But helping dispel fears and concerns is a cornerstone of parenting a child. Dr. Susan Bartell breaks it all down in a straightforward yet lighthearted manner to help parents master this very important skill."

—Danielle Sullivan, managing editor
of *NY Metro Parents*

"Dr. Susan Bartell has done it again! She takes the toughest questions that kids ask us parents and gives us clear steps to figure out how we'll answer *before* the questions are asked. Using her recommendations will deepen communication and understanding between children and parents."

—Nancy Gruver, founder of New Moon
Girl Media and author of *How to Say It to Girls*

"Easy-to-implement parenting advice in bite-sized, easy-to-read pieces. Dr. Bartell states the question, uncovers the meaning, and suggests how to respond."

—Lucy Banta, managing editor of
New Jersey Family and *Raising Teens*

THE TOP 50 Questions

KIDS ASK

• Pre-K through 2nd Grade •

The Best Answers
to the Toughest,
Smartest, and
Most Awkward
Questions Kids
Always Ask

DR. SUSAN BARTELL

sourcebooks

Published by Sourcebooks, Inc.
P.O. Box 4410, Naperville, Illinois 60567-4410
(630) 961-3900
Fax: (630) 961-2168
www.sourcebooks.com

Library of Congress Cataloging-in-Publication Data

Bartell, Susan.
  The top 50 questions kids ask (pre-K through 2nd grade) : the best answers to the toughest, smartest, and most awkward questions kids always ask / Susan Bartell.
       p. cm.
  1. Children's questions and answers. I. Title.
  HQ784.Q4B372 2010
  649'.123—dc22

                    2009039238

Printed and bound in the United States of America.
VP 10 9 8 7 6 5 4 3 2 1

For my children, Max, Gillian, and Mollie.
You started asking questions as soon as you
could talk, and I hope you never stop!

For every child and parent with
whom I have ever worked.
Your questions have taught me how to help
kids be happy, and I am deeply grateful.

Contents

Acknowledgments

This book could not have been written without the hundreds and hundreds of questions that were submitted by parents from every state and from countries as far away as England and Australia, and as close as Jamaica and Canada. I thank each one of you for responding to my request for questions and even more so for forwarding my request to other moms and dads. Your children's questions really were a window into your lives—some made me cry, others let me see the exasperation that all kids can evoke, and a few were so funny I laughed until I cried. Whether or not I used your question, each submission helped to inform and shape my writing, so you have my deepest gratitude.

Once again, I want to thank my editor at Sourcebooks, Sara Appino. This is our second project together, and

Sara continues to prove herself to be insightful, clear-thinking, and hard-working. I appreciate her advocacy of my work and her enthusiastic personality.

As with every book I write, I consider having the opportunity to write a luxury that I wouldn't have been able to achieve without the support of my family. My children, Max, Gillian, and Mollie, are my constant cheering team—I couldn't be a luckier mom, and I love you to the moon, to the stars, to Brooklyn, and back again.

My parents and my mother-in-law, aside from telling me (and anyone else who will listen) how proud they are of me, offer consistent, practical help with anything and everything—whenever I ask. I am truly grateful to have your support, and I love you.

If you know me at all, you will realize that my last thank-you always goes to my husband Lewis. This is because if I started with him, there wouldn't be space for anyone else on the page. We always work together as a team to support each other's important life projects, and this one is no exception. Lew, I don't have the words to thank you for your continued dedication to me and to our family. You are my never-ending love.

Susan Bartell, PsyD

March 2010

Introduction

Moms and dads can't wait for their kids to start talking—it's one of the greatest thrills of our parenting lives. But I'm sure you'll agree that when the never-ending questions start coming, we sometimes wish our precious children had never learned the meaning of the words "why" and "what"—not to mention all the other words in between that seem to end in a question mark, strung together to form a question that doesn't even make sense all the time.

But guess what? While I absolutely acknowledge that the questions of preschool- and early-elementary-age children can be tedious, annoying, and relentless, during this stage of development your child's questions begin taking on a deeper value that can help you to understand his or her dreams, wishes, fears, and hopes—if only you can find the key to unlock their meaning.

By paying close attention to your child's questions, you can often learn how to scratch below the surface. Then, once you really have a great understanding of your child's questions, you can learn to respond to them in a way that will encourage your child to share even more with you, rather than end the conversation. In this way you are planting the seeds for a lifetime of excellent communication between you and your child.

Parents often tell me that they are frustrated because they don't know how to communicate fully with their children; they wish their kids would talk to them more. By learning how to respond to your child's questions differently, you will open up these lines of communication beginning now, while your child is still very young. You will then be able to build on this growing bond as your child gets older. By the time your child is a teenager, you will have nurtured a wonderful, close relationship—it doesn't get any better than that!

My purpose in *The Top 50 Questions Kids Ask* is to help you learn to become an expert—as good as any psychologist—at getting your child to communicate with you about his or her concerns, worries, and even happy moments. This is the perfect time to do it, just as your child is venturing into the world of expressive language. Beginning in preschool and then moving into the early elementary years, your child's eyes are opened to so many new experiences. At the same time, his ability to utilize language is growing in leaps and bounds. His questions now are more than just a couple of words strung together. They have real meaning. They can be a challenge to answer, and they can tell you so much about your child.

The questions in *The Top 50 Questions* are all *real* questions from parents just like you, from all over the United States and even other parts of the world. In fact, I received hundreds and hundreds of questions in response to an online request I generated. You're probably wondering how I decided which questions to include and which ones to leave out. Actually, it was quite a simple decision. Just as there are predictable physical growth patterns that occur during the preschool and early elementary years, the cognitive and emotional changes in your child's life will also take a predictable path, and this will be reflected in the type of questions he or she asks. Based on this, it may not come as a surprise to you to learn that many of the submissions I received from parents were similar. The most common question I received for this age group was, "Can I have a snack?" Does that surprise you? Not me! Little kids love snack time—it's a central part of their brand-new school life. What's more, they're so busy all the time that they constantly need refueling to keep up their energy. But I'll talk more about snack time in Chapter One.

The selection process for *The Top 50 Questions* was based on which questions I received most frequently from parents with children in the preschool through second grade range. It was that simple—and that complicated. I have to admit, there were some questions that I absolutely loved—they made me laugh, cry, or think really hard—but because they didn't reflect the most frequently received questions, I couldn't include them. I wished I could—I was really tempted to—but I didn't.

However, if you submitted questions, and now you are reading this book and don't see your child's question, don't think for a second I didn't consider yours. I read each and every question and struggled mightily with which ones to include. Every one touched me. Every one made me think of the child, the parent, and the family that was behind it. Wow, there are a lot of really wonderful, really struggling, really interesting, really hard-working, really busy, and really tired families out there!

While reading this book, it's important for you to always keep in mind that just as with physical growth, the range of "normal" for emotional, social, cognitive, and academic growth is huge, which is why *The Top 50 Questions* covers preschool all the way through second grade—one child may ask a question in preschool, but another child may not be ready to ask the very same question until second grade. Both are normal, regular kids. In fact, if you have a child at the older end of this age range, you'll really enjoy reading *The Top 50*

Questions Kids Ask (3rd through 5th Grade). You'll find that your second-grade child may already be asking third-grade questions, so you'll be happy to have the next book as a resource.

You may be wondering why I've included preschool in this book, along with the early elementary grades. The truth is that, developmentally, preschoolers and kindergartners are more similar than they are different. The fact that kindergartners may be in different schools (although not always) is not as important as the fact that developmentally they are much more similar to early-elementary-age children than they are to nursery-school-age children. Many preschoolers are learning to read and write, and they are starting to seek independence socially. They fit in this grouping very well, which you will find as you begin reading.

Of course, some children can actually be much less or much more sophisticated than their peers when it comes to questions or any other area of emotional development. When this happens, a parent may begin worrying that his or her child's behavior seems to be too different from the way other children are behaving. If this seems to describe your child—if you have any concerns that your child is somehow "behind" or even too far ahead developmentally, cognitively, or socially, it's important not to ignore it. Speak to your child's medical doctor, teacher, school counselor, or a child psychologist or social worker. If there is a problem, the earlier you address it, the better it is for your child—and for you.

Now, by taking a quick glance at the Table of Contents, you will see that the questions are divided into nine chapters. I have chosen these chapters carefully to represent the most important areas of emotional and cognitive development for children in the preschool and early elementary school grades. As you read *The Top 50 Questions*, these chapters will make sense to you. You will find yourself nodding in agreement as you see your child reflected in the questions (even if you didn't submit a single one of them), and then as you begin to understand the best ways to respond to each question, it will again make sense and will feel natural and easy for you.

In fact, none of this is going to feel like hard work. Your child is asking you the questions anyway. All you will need to learn how to do is tweak your responses so that you answer in a way that will actually strengthen and deepen your relationship with your child and also reduce your own frustration. In addition, you will learn to respond to your child's questions in a way that will truly meet her cognitive and emotional needs. By responding differently and meeting these needs, you will begin to decrease the "nag, nag, nag" factor and understand your child just a little bit better than you did before you began reading. Sounds good, right? Well, I think we're ready to begin.

As always, I love to hear from those who read my books, so feel free to email me at DrSusan@DrSusanBartell. com. Send me more questions too if you like, and maybe the next book will include yours.

Happy answering!

Dr. Susan

Nag, Nag, Nag

Admit it, when you held your beautiful newborn child in your arms, you had no idea that one day you would be pulling out your hair because you heard the same question for about the billionth time that day. I know that nobody prepared me for this part of parenting! Perhaps parents keep it a secret so that they don't scare off the parents-to-be.

Children are experts at nagging—better than anyone I know. But sometimes I wonder if they learn from us nagging them. "Pick up your toys...Don't argue...Stop wriggling...Listen to me." We may not realize it, but we parents are pretty good naggers too, and *kids learn best from behaviors that are modeled for them*. This is my first psychological message for you. So keep it in mind as we go through this chapter and the rest of the book.

In fact, I'm going to ask you to call on some of your own feelings as we explore your child's nagging questions throughout the chapter.

Nagging is an interesting phenomenon. It is employed by a child who feels that his needs or wants are not being met. He hopes that by asking over and over, he will eventually change your initial response from a no to a yes. Now, let me pose a couple of questions to you:

- How does this nagging make you feel?
- How do you typically respond when your child nags?
- Do you find that your response to the nagging has resulted in your child nagging less?

As we explore your child's nagging questions, keep my questions in mind. You might find that your approach to your child's questions needs to change in order to get your child to nag less and for you to feel less frustrated.

Most parents feel incredibly frustrated, angry, or worn-down when their children nag. Their response, therefore, is typically one that they hope will end the nagging as quickly as possible: to yell and scream, give in to the request, or ignore the child altogether. Which do you do most of the time?

The truth is that none of these is especially effective at stopping nagging in its tracks. Yelling might temporarily stop your child, but he'll likely start nagging again once he's over the initial fear of your reprimand; giving in will simply reinforce the nagging (much more on this later in the chapter), and ignoring your child altogether doesn't address the nagging at all and will definitely increase your child's frustration that his question isn't being addressed. Instead, it is important to address the nagging head-on with effective techniques. Reading this chapter carefully will teach you how to do that. Now we're ready to tackle the questions.

#1: HOW MUCH LONGER?
(OR: ARE WE THERE YET?)

Lillian, mother of Mallory (age 4½), explained her frustration: "Every single time, as we are leaving somewhere—no matter where we are going—Mal will ask me, 'Mommy, how long will it take?' I will say, 'About fifteen minutes,' and then three minutes later she'll ask, 'Are we nearly there?' It drives me crazy!"

It doesn't seem to matter if you're on a twenty-minute drive or a four-hour trip, young children can't stand being in the car, plane, train, or bus, even with all the electronics we can now offer them to stay amused (for which most parents are extremely thankful). This question might be accompanied by whining, kicking the back seat, or bickering with a sibling.

It's safe to say that, for parents, it's important to find a way to respond to it in a way that will encourage less nagging and more cooperative behavior.

Uncovering the Meaning

Like Mallory, children in the preschool and early elementary years haven't yet developed an accurate sense of time. The younger the child, the poorer her concept of how long it takes to get somewhere. For this reason, telling your child, "It will take us about fifteen minutes to get to the store," or "We'll be at the beach in four hours, depending on traffic," could sound like pig Latin, but not as much fun. This is typically why kids nag so much while you're on a long trip—or even a short one. Since your initial time frame didn't mean very much to them, they're hoping that each time they ask again (and again and again), you'll say something that resembles English to them and that also sounds promising (i.e., "We're almost there").

In addition, the longer the trip, without a real sense of what the time frame means, the more likely your child is to become bored, anxious, and restless, resulting in the negative behaviors and nagging questions. This is particularly true when your child feels really cooped up—like when she is seat-belted in a car (or a bus or plane).

Restless behavior, aside from simply being your child's way of expending energy when she's in a tight environment, can also be her way of trying to engage you—in other words, get your attention. Do you consider your car your "haven"—at least when you are alone? Many parents find being in the car a time when they can relax, listen to some music, and unwind a little bit.

I have a confession to make—I love long car trips. My husband, kids, and best friends Julie and Rich think I'm certifiably crazy, but I find car trips relaxing and adventurous. However, even *I* would not enjoy a long car trip ruined by bickering, whining, nagging children.

If you're like me, you might hope that your child (or children) will take care of herself while you relax during a drive—short or long. Your child probably sees things a bit differently. She wants to talk to you, sing a song, or play a game. Her nagging questions are a way to keep you connected to her if she sees that you are reluctant to stay engaged.

In order to make car rides a little less boring for your child and much less stressful for you, the right type of response to your child's question will really help.

The Best Way to Respond

I came to the conclusion a long time ago—as you will have to do as well—that when my children are in the car, it is not a time to relax. It is, however, a time to really enjoy their company, particularly because there are no other distractions. You will be shocked—in a happy way—at how the nagging, bickering, and other negative behavior will be reduced, if you simply stay connected and engaged with your child during a car ride. For short rides, you should have a few songs ready to sing and quick games to play, like "I spy" or "let's spell a word." For longer rides, you will need to plan a bit better. Your repertoire will need to include many more songs to sing, stories to tell, CDs to listen to together, games to play, and whatever other ways you can think of that will keep you and your child engaged for the necessary amount of time.

You might not be surprised to learn that being patient in addition to preparation is definitely a crucial part of this situation—no matter how many times your child has asked you this question. For one thing, you're stuck in the car (plane or train) together, and if you get cranky (along with your child), it will make the situation even worse.

Next, the best way to respond to the question itself is to give your child an estimation of how much longer the trip will take within a time frame that makes sense in her world. Be creative! Your child will not only learn a sense of time, but will have fun doing it. For example, try the following responses:

- "This trip will take as long as eight TV shows— with commercials. Which TV shows do you think it should be?"
- "We will be there in about as long as circle time lasts in school. What circle time songs do you want to sing?"
- "Pretend you're eating dinner; that's about how long it will take."

It's also important to be as clear and concrete as possible. "I'm not sure," "still a little while," "ask Daddy," "soon," and "a few more minutes" are all too vague and will elicit continued, frequent nagging. Instead try, "We still have about two more hours, which is four TV shows, left to go. I'll tell you again when it's one hour—which would be two TV shows. In the meantime, let's play the license plate game/have a snack/draw a picture." For a shorter trip, you can say, "We have twenty minutes, which is about as long as it takes to get undressed, put your clothes in the hamper, take a bath, get out, and put on your PJs. In ten minutes, I'll tell you to get out of the bath, and then you'll know we're halfway there."

Last, anticipating and preparing for this question are extremely important. You'll be much less likely to be the victim of nagging—especially on long trips—if you truly prepare well for them.

When you are driving, plan for many rest stops—to use the bathroom and for snacks or meals. I would estimate adding an average of fifteen minutes for every two hours of travel time. If you plan for this in advance, you won't feel stressed or behind schedule when it happens. In fact, you will actually feel more relaxed because your child will have time to stretch her legs and won't feel as cooped up. For all types of trips, make sure you have enough food and travel games and toys to keep your child occupied.

Most important, don't expect that this trip will be relaxing for you. Traveling with young children takes effort—you need to entertain them. This is particularly true when you are traveling on public transportation.

It is your duty as a parent to make sure your child (or children) is not annoying other passengers. While this may be hard work for you, it is your choice to travel with your child; it is not the other passengers' choice to be inconvenienced by whining, screaming, nagging, or frenetic kids. The more you plan in advance, the less your child will nag, the more pleasant she will be, and the less stressed you will be by the experience.

#2: WILL YOU PLAY WITH ME?
(OR: I'M BORED, WHAT SHOULD I DO?)

I'm happy to say that my children are eleven, thirteen, and fifteen, and they still ask me to play with them. Sometimes I say yes, and sometimes I tell them I don't have time right at that moment. But as you can imagine, at this stage, they don't rely on me to play with them all the time.

Melissa tells a different story: "Joey (age 5) wants me to play with him all the time. He can't seem to amuse himself at all, and unless I let him watch TV or play video games, he's nagging me to play with him. I love spending time with him, but I really want him to learn to occupy himself at least some of the time, without an electronic baby-sitter, especially when I have to do something like pay the bills or feed the baby. Am I expecting too much of him?"

Like Melissa, many parents of preschool- and early-elementary-age children feel that their kids don't know how to occupy themselves. Like her, they're not sure if they should be responding to this question by saying, "No, this time you find something to play by yourself," or whether that's simply too harsh at such a young age.

But don't worry if you don't yet have the correct answer. The fact that you are thinking about it means you're taking the most important step. By the end of this section, you'll know what to do.

Uncovering the Meaning

When your child frequently asks you to play with him or seems bored all the time, he is likely telling you one or more of the following things:

- He wants your attention.
- Choosing an activity is difficult for him.
- He doesn't know how to play by himself.

Let's examine these one at a time.

If your child *wants your attention*, it is either because you don't spend enough time with him or because there is something going on in your family that is making him feel he needs extra attention. Ask yourself if either of these is the case. Do you work very long hours? Do you socialize a great deal? Do you spend a lot of time on the phone or computer during the time you could be with your child? Do you have a new baby that is getting most of your attention? Are you divorcing or is there other turmoil in your family? Any of the above could make your child feel that he wants and needs some exclusive time with you (and rightly so).

A child does need extra attention when he is going through a particularly rough patch. However, sometimes you may be going through a tough time at the exact same time as your child (during a divorce, for example), making it very difficult for you to have the emotional energy to give to your child. Being aware of this is important. If you don't have the necessary strength to meet your child's emotional needs, you may need to ask for help from your support system or from a professional—for you and your child.

Some children *find it difficult to choose an activity to play alone*. They always want to play with someone else because they rely on the other person to guide the play. Since a young child usually has a parent—rather than any other adult—around most often, you're typically the person he asks (and asks, and asks) to play with him. In addition, if you work, your childcare provider probably spends a lot of time playing with your child. Of course, this is what you have hired her to do, so you don't want her to *not* play with your child—she's doing her job well. But, at the same time, a very attentive full-time baby-sitter tends to reduce the independence of the child in her care, simply because she is such a willing participant and would never say no, unless she needed to take care of another child in the family.

Other kids may know how to choose a game, but once the game is chosen, they *don't know how to play alone*. Perhaps they don't feel creative enough, they don't find the game exciting enough with only themselves involved, they don't like to be alone, or they get bored or frustrated easily. Some children's personalities are well-matched to playing alone. They can sit for hours building, coloring, creating, or pretending. But many children can't or won't. They seem to only find joy in the act of play when another person is engaged with them.

But does understanding the underlying meaning of this question mean that you should always play with your child when he nags you five times a day to do so? No, it doesn't.

The Best Way to Respond

Teaching your child to play by himself is actually an important life skill. By learning to play alone, your child will learn the skill of self-soothing. You will hear me discuss this term in other places in this book. It is one of the psychological concepts that are *very* important to know when it comes to understanding your child's development. Children who can soothe themselves are able to reduce their own feelings of frustration when they are confronted with situations they don't like. As you can imagine this is important not only when it comes to learning to play alone, but in school, socially, and throughout life. An adult who has a temper tantrum when a supermarket line doesn't move fast enough probably wasn't taught self-soothing skills as a young child. A teenager who screams at the teacher when he fails a math test has also probably not learned self-soothing skills. Helping your child learn to cope with frustration by meeting his own needs is a critical life skill. Learning how to play alone is a part of this.

There are two exceptions to encouraging your child to play by himself:

- When you do an honest assessment of your behavior, you realize that you do not spend enough time playing with your child. In this case, you will need to start spending more time playing with your child.
- If your child is going through a rough adjustment to a change, he may be feeling especially needy. In this instance, you may need to spend extra time playing with your child, even if you already do spend an adequate amount of time playing with him.

In all other cases, the best way to respond to this question is to say this to your child:

1. "Pick two things you can do by yourself." (If he can't pick, then help him.)
2. "Choose one of them to do by yourself."
3. "You need to play this by yourself until the timer goes off. If you want, you can switch to the other

one, but you need to play by yourself the whole time." (Set a timer for fifteen minutes; if this is too long, start with ten minutes. Gradually work up to thirty minutes.)

At the end, offer your child praise and compliments for playing alone. This way he will feel that he's receiving your attention even though you didn't play with him. Do not expect a child this age (especially a boy) to play alone for longer than thirty minutes. If yours does, consider yourself lucky!

#3: CAN I HAVE A SNACK?
(OR: CAN I HAVE A DRINK?)

This was the number-one question I received in any category for this age group. Just about every single submission contained it in some form or another. Dominic (age 7), Angie (age 5), and Celia (age 3) ask their mom, Angela, this question all day long. "I feel like they've barely finished a meal, and they're already asking me for a snack. How could they possibly be hungry already? I never know whether to give them one or to make them wait."

I'm sure you know the feeling too. Kids nag about food more than just about anything else. But with the rate of childhood obesity at an all-time high, we can't simply give our kids snacks every time they ask. Furthermore, we also have to think about why they ask so often, especially if they are not really hungry.

Uncovering the Meaning

Of course little kids are hungry sometimes and do need snacks—they expend a lot of energy playing, learning, and growing. In addition, as I mentioned in the introduction to the book, snacks are a part of the culture of early childhood. They are an integral part of both preschool and the early elementary grades. Kids discuss what snack they are bringing to school, they compare and share snacks, and they are always looking for a more interesting snack to brag about to their friends.

However, when we began this chapter, I mentioned that kids learn best from behaviors that are modeled for them. This is true whether the modeled behavior is healthy or unhealthy. When it comes to food, adults often model unhealthy eating habits for their children. For example, perhaps your child asks for snacks a hundred times a day because she sees you snacking all day long. Or maybe you have a huge, irresistible snack closet stuffed full of junk food.

Here's another good psychological tip for you. Children will continue to engage in (and even increase) positive or negative behaviors that are reinforced. This means that if you give your child a snack every time she asks for one, she will keep nagging you for snacks (the *negative behavior* is asking, and when you give her the snack you *reinforce* that behavior). It *is* hard to say no, but it's more difficult to break bad habits later in your child's life. It's especially challenging to help an overweight child lose weight.

Another behavior that parents sometimes model without realizing it is using snack food to manage feelings. We may eat when we are happy, sad, angry, and bored. Then we pass this on to our kids by giving them snacks for the same reasons. Even if we don't model it, in the preschool and early elementary years, a child will often ask for a snack because she's bored. By giving in and offering her food, you don't allow her the opportunity to spend her time differently. We discussed self-soothing and frustration tolerance—here it is again. Food is not a healthy way to soothe one's feelings. It leads to unhealthy weight gain and to the use of food to manage feelings. This is the time to teach your child that snacks are just like meals—to be eaten when you're hungry.

The Best Way to Respond

Before responding to this question, you need to prepare your child by setting up household "snack rules." If you don't have rules about snacks in your home, it's important to make them. If you do have rules, this is the time to reinforce them. The rules should contain the following components:

- You get one *healthy* snack for school (or two, depending on what your school requires). Healthy snacks do not include candy, cookies, cake, or other sugary snacks.
- You get one healthy after-school snack.
- You can have one small, less healthy ("junk food") snack each day, either after school or after dinner.
- If you are still hungry between meals, fruit or veggies are the only choice. If you refuse these (or, for children who really won't eat fruit/veggies, another truly healthy food like a slice of cheese or chicken breast), you need to wait until the next meal. (Your child won't starve, I promise you.)

You are now armed and ready to respond to the question. It's that simple—all you need to do is follow the rules. If your child can read, I recommend that you post the rules in the kitchen. If not, you simply need to remind your child of them verbally. It's important not to make exceptions—remember what we discussed about reinforcing behaviors. Once you start reinforcing this new set of behaviors, the nagging for a snack will diminish and possibly (if you're really lucky!) vanish altogether. If you really feel that your child's eating is out of control and you can't seem to manage it yet, or if your child is already showing signs of being overweight, I strongly recommend you get a copy of my book *Dr. Susan's Fit and Fun Family Action Plan*. It will teach you everything you need to know about getting your child and your whole family living a healthy and happy life in a positive and upbeat way.

I hope it doesn't escape you that you can use this same set of techniques—planning, consistency, and reinforcement—to encourage positive (and discourage negative) behaviors of any kind. During these early years, setting up this type of parenting is important because it will help you raise a well-behaved child that you and everyone else will like.

- -

#4: WHY CAN'T I HAVE DONUTS FOR BREAKFAST?
(OR: WHY CAN'T I EAT CANDY ALL THE TIME?)

- -

Yes, this is another food question. But you'll soon see that the meaning behind it is completely different than the prior question. Darnel (age 6½) is not an easy kid. His parents, Kevin and Charity, say that he argues about many things. But, they explain, "Darnel's most frequent question is, 'How come I can't have cake for breakfast?' He won't take no for an answer, and we don't know what to tell him."

From an adult perspective, this question (and similar ones) seems to have a perfectly reasonable answer: "You can't have donuts for breakfast because it's not healthy for you." But your gut feeling tells you that even at four or five years old, your child doesn't need to be told this. So why is he asking the question? There must be more to it, right?

Uncovering the Meaning

Right! Most children do know by now that donuts, cake, and cookies would not make a healthy breakfast. They also know that eating candy all day long would not be healthy. In fact, they would likely be upset and disturbed if you gave in to their nagging and allowed them to eat this unhealthily for more than a day or so. But yet they keep nagging. Why?

Children (of all ages) have an inborn mandate to constantly test and challenge the limits set for them. It may drive you crazy, but it is a healthy part of growing up. *It is your job to stand firm on the important boundaries and only give in on the minor ones. This is how you teach your child to feel both safe and independent at the same time.* So, like Darnel, many preschool- and early-elementary-age kids argue with their parents about healthy eating. It gives them the opportunity to practice flexing their muscles of independence in an arena with which they are very familiar—food—while feeling comforted that mom or dad will continue to make the right choices to keep them healthy—even if they don't like it.

Of course, if your child has gone to someone's home where they *do* eat donuts or cake for breakfast, then perhaps he is asking you this question because he genuinely wants to know why that family is allowed to eat it in that home, but he is not allowed to in his home. Nevertheless, the message you give your child needs to have the same level of consistency and commitment to what you consider healthy for your child and your family. What other people do in their homes has nothing to do what you do in your family. In fact, this is an opportunity to teach your child that even adults do not give in to peer pressure. At the same time, you want to be careful not to appear too judgmental, or your child may be afraid to tell you when he does eat food that he thinks you may be disapproving of.

The Best Way to Respond

Your response to this question needs to take into account the issue with which your child is grappling—wanting to feel independent, while still hoping that you will take care of him. Begin by asking your child why he thinks he can't have donuts for breakfast. With any luck, he'll give you the right answer, and you'll be able to simply tell him he's absolutely right and move on from there.

However, if he says he doesn't know, wants you to tell him, or insists that there is nothing wrong with donuts for breakfast (or candy all day long), you can respond with a version of the following: "It is my job to make sure you are healthy, inside and out. Eating donuts for breakfast won't give you enough healthy energy to think, learn, and play for the day. But, you can choose whether you want cereal, eggs, or grilled cheese for breakfast." As you can see, the response shows your child that you are taking care of him but at the same time allowing him some independence in his breakfast choice.

If he has seen or eaten an unhealthy "breakfast of champions" in someone else's home, you might want to add: "It's fine for you to eat it as a special treat at someone else's house, and we don't judge what other people do, but in our family, we choose healthier food."

You can employ a similar response if your child asks why he can't eat candy all the time: "Eating candy all the time can give you cavities, and it doesn't give your body good energy for thinking and playing. But you can have one small 'junk food' snack a day. Would you like that to be a small piece of candy?"

#5: WHY?

"'But, why, Mommy? Why, why, why?' is what I hear a hundred times a day from Ava (age 4½)," explained her frustrated mom, Nancy. "I don't think she even cares if I answer her. She asks the question over and over, whenever I tell or ask her to do anything. Sometimes, as I begin answering one 'why,' she's already asking another one about my explanation. It's a constant nagging at me."

Many parents of young children feel just like Nancy, plagued with the open-ended, seemingly meaningless question, "Why?" They are not sure how to teach their children to stop asking it or, better yet, to ask it only once in a while, when they are truly interested in knowing the answer to a specific question.

Uncovering the Meaning

"Why?" is a powerful question for a young child. In fact, it is probably the first question that most toddlers learn to ask. It's a short word, easy to pronounce, and it causes an adult to gleefully engage with the adorable child immediately as she attempts to respond. This attention reinforces the youngster to keep asking, "Why, why, why?" In these very early years of language development, your child didn't understand that she was asking a question, nor did she comprehend your response, other than the fact that she was getting your attention.

As she grows older, though, and her capacity for language improves, your child inevitably recognizes that "Why?" is a question requiring a response. In some cases, she will ask a real "why" question because she really wants to clarify something confusing or gain a greater understanding as to why she cannot do something she wants to do. However, there are still remnants of the desire for attention from when she was a younger child. At these times, she will ask "why" without really thinking, simply to engage you in conversation or to elicit a response from you, even if it is an impatient or aggravated response: "Because I said so, that's why!"

At other times, her "why" is a result of her not getting her way. This is more of an aborted anger response than a real curiosity. Rather than yelling or lashing out at you in a manner she knows is socially unacceptable, she will nag, whine, and moan, "But whhhhyyyyy????" Despite your rational explanations, she will continue in this manner, until you either give in or become angry.

The Best Way to Respond

As with all other nagging behaviors, immediately giving in to the "why" question every single time will definitely reinforce it—meaning *more* nagging in your direction. In order to teach your child to be more thoughtful about when she asks you "why," you will want to begin challenging her to use her own brain to answer the question for herself sometimes. There is a simple formula for doing this. Every single time she asks you "why," respond by saying, "Why do *you* think?" You might be surprised to find out that most of the time she will know the answer to the question she asked you. Doing this will serve four purposes:

1. It will take your child off "why" auto-pilot.
2. It will show you and your child that she knows more than you think she does.
3. It will make your child exercise her brain, rather than rely on you to provide her with all the answers.

4. It will increase conversation between you and your child, because if she really doesn't know the answer to a "why" question, you and she can discuss it until she discovers the answer.

Getting Out in the World

For a preschool- or elementary-age child (and her parents), going to school, beginning to explore extracurricular activities, and starting to spend time with peers as friends, offer the first real opportunities for truly meaningful social interaction, as well as the chance to explore rules and routines outside her own home and outside of the presence of a parent.

Even for kids who have already been in nursery school or day care, the more advanced cognitive development of this age group allows a child to face the challenges of his new social world differently than he has before. The questions your child asks during this stage reflect this newfound desire to explore and challenge the boundaries of his world.

However, the questions are also a sign of something more: the beginning of a sense that disappointment is sometimes an unpleasant fact of life. When we explore the questions concerning fears in Chapter Four, you will begin to see that, developmentally, children in this age range become acutely aware of the fact that the world is not perfect and that bad things can happen—therefore they naturally develop fears and need to learn how to master them. Here in Chapter Two, you will notice that as your child becomes more socially connected to peers and more challenged by schoolwork, the questions she asks reflect this same feeling that managing the ups and downs of life is complicated and not always fun and games. There are many ways for you to learn to understand and respond to her questions. Mastering these will help her overcome her challenges in the best ways possible. As you explore the questions in this chapter you will learn many new and interesting ideas about how to help your child negotiate her ever-expanding world.

#6: CAN I PLAY WITH A FRIEND?

Victoria told me that her daughter Katie (age 6) wakes up every morning, and before brushing her teeth, she has already asked if she can play with someone that day. "Katie will say, 'Mommy, can you call to see if Andi can play, or Heather or Jaime? Please, Mommy, please?' Unless I promise to do my best to try and get someone for her to play with, she's frustrated and upset."

You may find that as your child becomes more social, she will ask this question daily—whether it is a school day or weekend. There seems to be little regard for whether there is actually time in the day to play with a friend, or whether you are able to arrange it within your schedule or the schedule of the other child's parent. The drive to be with friends becomes stronger and stronger as children enter this stage of development. It is almost as if now that they've tasted what it's like to have a social life, they can't get enough of it.

Uncovering the Meaning

This question represents the first sign that your child is now behaving as a full-fledged, independently functioning, social human being. Your child will meet new friends primarily in school and at extra-curricular activities. She will learn how to make friends and interact with them, with less parent or teacher involvement than when she was younger. She will thrill at the opportunity to build on these new relationships outside of school—thus the continued nagging question.

Some kids want to be outside playing ball all day long, while others want to be tucked away in their bedrooms chatting and playing board games with their friends. Not only is getting along with a friend a newfound skill that your child realizes she can do really well, but it feels great to have someone to play with who isn't a parent or a sibling. It's an opportunity to learn new games and to explore different parts of her personality than she gets to explore in her family. Do you remember reading in Chapter One that some children don't like to play alone? Well, having a peer to play with ensures that they won't have to—at least some of the time—especially in a busy home where parents and siblings don't always have time to play.

Of course, as I will always remind you, like everything else, there is a range of normal social behavior among children. There are many completely well-adjusted children who are perfectly happy with one or two close friends, who have no need for constant social interactions, and who enjoy downtime alone when school is over. If your child does not ask to play with friends outside of school, it does not mean that something is wrong, unless he meets one or more of the following criteria. In this case, it's important to speak to your child's doctor, a child psychologist, or other mental health provider experienced in working with young children. It may simply mean that your child is shy, but if he is beginning to show signs of struggling socially, the earlier you provide intervention the better. Speak to a professional if your child

- avoids social interaction, shuts down, or becomes anxious around other children
- can interact socially with adults, but struggles to fit in with other kids
- doesn't have any friends, or is often left out, teased, or bullied

- is physically aggressive, verbally abusive, mean, or angry toward other children
- shows no interest at all in making friends or shies away from social interaction, one-on-one or in groups
- would like to make friends, but doesn't seem to know how to do it; despite you or the teacher helping, your child still can't figure out how to approach or interact with other kids in a way that they welcome

You should also seek help if your child's teacher or other school administrator has recommended that you do so.

The Best Way to Respond

There are two issues that you need to address when responding to this question. The first is to try to reduce the nag factor in order to preserve your own sanity. The second is to address your child's desire to have the social interaction she desires.

In Chapter One, we discussed the importance of being clear with your child about your expectations and then following through in order to reduce nagging questions. (You might want to take another quick look at Chapter One now, but don't forget to come back again.)

When it comes to socializing, it is a great idea to set up rules now, when your child is just starting out, because it's much more difficult to make rules for older children. In order to help your child learn the "rules" of socializing, you will need to do a little advance work. Your rules should include the following components:

1. All homework and other activities must be completed before any playtime can be planned.

2. You need to be asked (*not* told), before your child schedules a playdate with a friend. This is an important rule because some kids, especially girls, will begin to arrange their own social lives beginning at quite a young age.

3. Your child needs to give you at least one day (or more if you need it) to try and schedule time with a friend, and she can't be angry or upset if it doesn't work out. You need to explain that you don't control other people's schedules. Tell your child that an inappropriate response can result in a negative consequence.

Once the rules are established, it is much easier to respond to this question. Tell your child: "Yes, I will call Heather's mom and see if she's available tomorrow or the next day. Remember, it's too complicated to schedule playtime for the same day. When you come home from school today, I'll let you know if I have been able to arrange it. But don't forget, I'm not in charge of Heather's schedule, so I'll do my best, but it's not okay for you to be angry with me if it doesn't work out."

If the playdate doesn't work out and your child has a fit, I'd recommend a consequence that is related to her social life. For example: "Remember I told you that there would be a consequence if you were mad at me if the playtime with Heather didn't work out. Well, it's not okay that you're yelling and crying right now. It means that you won't be able to play with anyone for the next four days." Then make sure that *you follow through with the consequence or it will be meaningless.*

#7: WHY DOESN'T ALEX WANT TO BE MY FRIEND ANYMORE?

In stark contrast to the previous question, this one is a heartbreaker when you hear it for the first time (or for the tenth). Lydia and Tom were eating dinner when their son Adam (age 7½), with tears in his eyes, asked them, "How come Christopher won't let me play soccer with him anymore?" Lydia and Tom were surprised. Adam and Chris had been buddies since nursery school and they knew of no reason for anything to have changed.

"Did you have a fight with Chris?" asked Tom.

Adam shook his head forlornly. "No. I don't know; he told me that he was mad at me."

"Do you want me to talk to his mom?" suggested Lydia, hoping she could fix the problem.

"No way, Mom! I'll look like a baby. Don't talk to anyone!"

It is hard to believe that children experience social

difficulties like these beginning at such a young age. But since I received this question so many times as part of my survey, you can be sure that if your child is struggling socially in this way, he's not the only one, and you're not the only parent unsure of how to handle the question.

Uncovering the Meaning

Along with the positive aspects of making new friends, children also sometimes test out parts of their personalities that may not be as positive. Psychologically speaking, some children use new friendships as a way to express behaviors that have been role-modeled for them in their families. For example, if a child has a parent or older sibling who is bossy or critical, he may treat peers in this way. What's more, if a child feels that he is bullied, ignored, or criticized within his family system (by a sibling or parent), he may use his peer group as an opportunity to become the bully, to be mean, or to exclude a peer in order to turn around the feeling of powerlessness he experiences at home.

This doesn't mean that the child he chooses as his target (perhaps your child), should be forced to tolerate this behavior. For this reason, it is not always best to allow a child this young to handle all social difficulties alone—even if he insists on it. When a young child is bullied or ostracized, he does not recognize when adult intervention is necessary. When it becomes necessary, the best first response is typically to speak to the teacher (or school counselor), and not the other child's parent. This is because another parent might become defensive and the situation could become worse, rather than better. (As an aside, if you're told that your child is treating another child badly, it is not in your child's best interest to become defensive. Teaching your child to treat others respectfully is far more important than defending him if his behavior is wrong.)

However, bullying is not the only reason that a child chooses not to be friends with another child. In some instances, it is simply a matter of friendships changing as children grow and their interests change. For example, a nursery school friendship, cultivated and nurtured by the friendship of parents, may not continue once children are in elementary school. Although one child may want to continue the friendship, the other one may not feel as compelled. A new class full of potential new friends may make the old friendship less attractive, especially if the new kids seem to have more in common—an interest in a particular sport, game, or hobby, for example.

I have also learned over the years and through the many friendships of my three children that today's enemy can be tomorrow's best friend—and, of course, vice versa. While I was worrying, heartbroken, that my child was deeply distraught over a lost friendship, the fight was already over and the children were friends again. Usually the children work it out quickly and make up—sometimes more healthily than we adults ever do.

Young children, in particular, don't hold grudges. I wish we had the same philosophy as them.

In addition, I have learned, through my own children and through my work, that when it comes to a fight (this is not the case with bullying) it is never, ever solely the fault of the other child. No matter how upset your child may be, there are always two sides to a story. During the early elementary years, when children are notoriously poor at telling accurate stories, this is never truer. You will help your child grow as a person, and you will preserve many of your own friendships with the parents of your child's friends, when you keep this in mind. I now know to temper my feelings and take a "wait and see" attitude. I've slept better over the years for it.

The Best Way to Respond

Before offering a solution, ask your child the following questions (adapt the questions to your particular situation):

- How long has Chris been leaving you out?
- Did anything happen between you and him before he left you out?
- Have you tried to talk to him about it or ask the teacher for help?
- Is anyone else leaving you out/being mean to you?
- Who do you sit with at lunch and play with at recess?

These questions will help you assess whether the situation is new or whether it's been going on for a while already.

You will be able to assess whether your child has tried to do anything yet to resolve the situation and whether it is a problem beyond the one child. The last question is important because it will tell you specifically whether your child still has kids to be with during these critical times. He may not communicate this unless you ask it specifically.

Do not ask your child if he wants you to speak to the teacher or anyone else about the issue. If you assess that it has gone on for too long or has become a significant problem, tell him that you will talk to the teacher. If he becomes upset the way Adam did, tell him a version of the following: "It is not okay for a kid to be mean to another kid, and sometimes grown-ups need to get involved to fix the problem. I know you think you can do it yourself, but Chris needs an adult to help him see that being a bully is not acceptable."

If you believe that this is a short-term argument, or that your child can work it out alone or with you intervening by giving him suggestions only, then handle it this way first. Whenever possible, it is important for him to know that you believe in his ability to handle his problems for him and to see for himself that he can too. Remind him that everyone has arguments and that it doesn't mean the friendship is over. Encourage him to speak to his friend. No matter how upset you are, *resist the urge to take his side against the other child*. This will not help him resolve the issue, and in the likely case that they do make up, he will remember that you said negative things about his friend.

#8: CAN YOU HELP ME WITH MY HOMEWORK?
(OR: CAN THE BABY-SITTER/MY SISTER/MY BROTHER HELP ME WITH MY HOMEWORK?)

This question presents a dilemma for many parents because, more often than not, they are not sure how to answer it. Marcy's daughter Nicole (age 8) asks her for help every day. "I really want her to do her work independently, but she insists that I sit with her and help her, or she'll get it wrong and the teacher will be mad; and now my younger daughter Mae (age 5), whose only homework is usually to cut out pictures beginning with the letter of the day, wants me to help her too. I don't want Nicole to get into trouble, but I want to break this cycle."

Marcy's concern is understandable and similar to that of many parents. The concern you probably feel is that you don't want your child to be unable to complete a homework assignment because she doesn't know how to do it, but at the same time, you don't want her to rely on you to always help with homework. Some children (and parents) are also unsure how a teacher will treat a child who comes in with an incomplete homework assignment—even if the child did not understand the work. This is an important issue to resolve because bad habits are harder to break when children are older.

Uncovering the Meaning

Of course, if your child asks for help only occasionally, you should not be concerned. Everyone needs help with something once in a while. In this case, offer your help supportively, and then allow your child to move on alone.

Many teachers will ask that you not help your child with homework. They do this so that they will know when a child needs help with a particular part of the subject area that is being taught. Sometimes parents disregard this request, because they want their child to hand in "perfect" homework. By doing this, the message you send your child is that it is better to be correct than to learn from your mistakes. This is not useful for your child because she may become afraid to tell you when she really does need help, because she doesn't want to feel like a "failure" in your eyes. It doesn't benefit the teacher either, because she won't really have a good idea of what your child might not be able to do independently. It also puts you in the position of being trapped in always having to help your child, because you have now communicated to her that perfection is the goal. You will be helping from now through the end of her senior year of high school. And take it from me, the helping gets a lot harder as they get older. You might find yourself doing chemistry or calculus at midnight!

If your child is asking for your help on a regular basis, it is important to figure out what is causing it. There are three likely reasons this is happening:

1. She enjoys the one-on-one attention, but doesn't really require homework help.
2. You established the habit of sitting with her from the beginning, and now you don't want to do it anymore. However, your presence has become a crutch that she doesn't believe she can do without—and perhaps you're not sure she can either.
3. She is having difficulty with the academic demands of homework or with the attention/focus that homework requires. She truly needs you (or someone) there to explain the work to her or help her stay focused.

The Best Way to Respond

If your child asks for homework help because she likes the attention, it is best to begin weaning her from this. Respond by saying, "I'll sit with you and do my work/read, but you need to do your own work." After you have established this routine for a few weeks, you can then gradually shift by saying, "I'll sit with you for a few minutes, then I need to check on something, and I'll come back." Gradually your child will learn to work on her own.

If your presence has become a crutch to your child—she truly believes she needs your help, even if she doesn't—you should employ this same tactic. However, it may not be as easy to break away, because her level of anxiety will increase when you limit your willingness to help her. Begin by insisting that she do her easiest work alone first. Praise her independence. Gradually work toward her doing it all independently. Even the oldest children in this age range (second graders) don't typically receive a great deal of homework, and they should be able to fully achieve this shift toward independence within two or three weeks.

If your child truly struggles with homework, you need to address the problem differently. Continue to respond yes to your child and, at the same time, investigate what may be impacting on your child's difficulty doing homework independently. Is the work too hard for her? Does she have trouble concentrating, focusing, or staying on task? Does she become easily frustrated or confused? Are all subjects hard for her, or is it one particular area?

It is imperative that you immediately speak to her teacher and explain in specific detail what problems she is having at home that require your extra attention. Assess whether she is having these same difficulties in school. If she is, it is a good idea to request that the teacher offer some extra help to your child in order to try and address the issue.

If this doesn't work within a few weeks, I strongly suggest that you insist that your child's academic struggles be addressed at a meeting between you, the teacher, the school psychologist, and any other team members the teacher or school psychologist deems appropriate.

Do not wait to request this meeting. The school year flies by quickly, and the wheels of a school district's evaluative process turn very slowly—I assure you! Should your child require greater academic support, the sooner you begin, the better.

#9: WHY DO I HAVE TO GO TO SCHOOL?
(OR: DO I HAVE TO GO TO SCHOOL?)

It is usually surprising to hear this question asked by a preschool- or early-elementary-age child. Most young children love school, and it is puzzling for parents when they don't. Bianca and Eddie were upset when Eddie Jr. (age 5½) started showing resistance to attending kindergarten. He would drag his feet in the morning, make excuses, and say, "But why do I have to go to school? Why can't I stay home with you? Can I stay home for a couple of days; then I promise I'll go back?"

Although upsetting for a parent to hear, you might be surprised to learn that it is not unusual for young kids to go through phases—even long ones—when they ask why they have to go to school, or express a dislike of school. However, even though your child is young and you think that he will just get over this issue, the truth is that this is not a question you should ignore.

Uncovering the Meaning

If you take a look at *The Top 50 Questions Kids Ask (3rd through 5th Grade)*, you'll see a question called "Can I take a day off from school?" During this older developmental stage, a child has gained a more mature understanding and acceptance of how school fits into his life. However, in the preschool and early elementary years, a child may not yet have embraced the idea that school is here to stay—for a long time, whether or not he likes it. Therefore, when a child asks why he has to go to school, it may mean he is not enjoying school and would like it to end.

When you look at the prior question concerning homework help, it is understandable how a child who is struggling with schoolwork may not want to go to school each day. When a child has social difficulties (reread "Why doesn't Alex want to be my friend anymore?"), it can also cause him to want to avoid attending school.

But for some children, this question has another, less obvious, meaning. Here is an opportunity for me to share another psychological concept that I know you'll find interesting. For some young children, resistance to attending school actually has its genesis in a real difficulty leaving home, rather than not wanting to go to school. There can be many reasons for this including the following:

- If you've recently had a baby, your child may be jealous about leaving you home alone with the baby.

- If there is a lot of fighting in your family, he may be worried about going to school because he's afraid of what will happen while he's gone.
- If someone in your family is very ill, he could be anxious about leaving that person to go to school because he is deeply concerned that something very bad will happen to the person while he is away.

Interestingly, the opposite can also be true—a child can express homesickness when actually he doesn't want to go to school. For example, your child may say, "I'll miss you," "I'm afraid to leave you," or "I'll miss the baby," when the real issue is that he is struggling with his schoolwork. It is therefore important that you always speak to his teacher and never assume you know what is going on before you have the whole picture.

The Best Way to Respond

School phobia—the catchall term used to describe resistance to attending school (whether it is truly due to being afraid of school, or if it is due to not wanting to leave home)—can be very hard to eliminate once it takes hold. If you haven't experienced it already, you need to know that if you give even a tiny inch by letting your child have just one day off, you could be stuck with a daily temper tantrum for the rest of the school year. You also teach your child that running away from his problems is an acceptable solution, which it is not.

Therefore, the absolute best response is, "It is your job to go to school so that you can learn new, interesting things, and help your brain and body get stronger. If something is bothering you, or if you are having a hard time, we can talk about it, and I will help you fix it, but you need to go to school every single day."

Of course, it is necessary to try and figure out why your child is displaying this anxiety and then correct the situation. For example, if you have a new baby, you can make it clear that life at home is very boring while your child is in school. Perhaps draw a couple of pictures for your child or cook his favorite meal, and tell him you were thinking about him while he was in school. If there is family turmoil, it may be important to seek professional psychological help to assist you in coping or making changes so that your child is no longer negatively emotionally affected. Speaking to your child's school counselor in order to offer your child emotional support at school would also be helpful.

#10: IT'S NOT FAIR; HOW COME I NEVER WIN?
(OR: WHY CAN'T I WIN EVERY TIME?)

"Ella (age 6) is such a sore loser. She gets so upset when the other person wins." When I asked Lily,

Ella's mom, what most worried her about Ella's lack of graciousness about losing, she explained, "I'm worried that kids at school won't want to play with her if she always complains about losing. Kids don't like that."

Lily isn't wrong. Kids don't like it when their peers can't tolerate defeat. Nevertheless, many kids ask this question every day, because losing at a game or sport isn't easy and it doesn't feel good. However, not being the winner is a real part of every stage of life, from losing a game of Candyland when you're four years old to losing a basketball game when you're fourteen to losing a tennis tournament when you're thirty-four. The sooner you help your child to become accustomed to losing without frustration and anger, the better off your child will be socially.

So my question to you is, how do you respond to this question in a way that will help your child become a more gracious winner *and* loser, rather than always needing to win in order to feel good about herself?

Uncovering the Meaning

Young children, new to the world of socializing, haven't had much opportunity to practice managing uncomfortable feelings. True, some seem to be innately good at it; we observe the child who has no problem when she doesn't win, and in fact will keep a smile on her face, telling her opponent, "Good job," even when she loses over and over again. We admire such a temperament—most of us were not and will never be this even-tempered. Count your blessings if this is your child.

Most young kids struggle more than this—to one degree or another—to master feelings of failure, anger, and disappointment when they don't win. They take losing very personally at this young age, finding it difficult to separate their own self-worth from their achievement at the game, contest, or sport.

It is a parent's job to help a child learn to recognize the difference between being a "winner" as a person and merely winning at a sport or game. In fact, very often, the way you handle losing *makes* you a winner.

Sadly, sometimes, parents lose sight of this important message and convey a very different one to their children. I have observed many kids' sports events, for example, where a parent (most notably a father) cares only that his child—or her team—wins the game. If his child does not win or plays poorly in his eyes, he yells at the child or at the coach. There is little hope that this child (or a younger sibling observing this scene) will become anything but a sore loser herself. So as always, be aware of the behaviors you role-model for your child, beginning at a very young age.

In addition to being a good role model, sometimes a child struggles with being a good loser because her parents have, until now, protected her from losing. It can be tempting to let your child win at this age. After all, she's just learning how to play games, and she doesn't yet have the skill. Heck, you're a grown-up; of course you're going to beat her every time, unless you let her feel good and win. There's plenty of time to experience losing, and why should you be the bad guy?

The truth is, your child won't be able to learn how to manage her uncomfortable feelings about not winning if she isn't given the chance to experience them. And the best place for her to practice working through these feelings and managing them is with you, rather than with peers who may be much less tolerant. What's more, the longer you wait, the harder it becomes for your child to become good at being gracious at losing—whether it be at sports, board games, or any other activity. By four years old, your child should be actively working on the skills of being a gracious loser, and by five, you should be noticing these skills becoming much more strongly developed. If you are not yet seeing this in your child of this age or older, it's time to intervene.

The Best Way to Respond

When your child becomes upset about losing, you need to respond in a realistic, yet calm manner. The way you teach your child to cope well with losing is by allowing her to lose, rather than letting her win. This is true, even if you are afraid she will have an unpleasant reaction. In fact, it's particularly true if you think she won't cope well, because she needs a chance to learn to change her response.

Try saying something similar to the following: "Everyone wins sometimes and loses sometimes. Right now you may feel like you lose all the time, but you really don't. But it's not fun for me to play with you if you always complain about losing, and I bet kids at school don't like it either. Let's try and play the game again, but if you lose and then cry or have a tantrum, we're going to stop playing, and I won't play again with you until tomorrow."

If your child has a particularly unpleasant reaction— she gets angry, upset, or has a fit even when it appears that she's losing, or even when someone else scores even one point—you should stop the activity immediately. Tell your child you aren't having fun, and you aren't going to play with her anymore unless she can be happy or even pretend to be happy for you (or the person with whom she is playing). If your child ends the activity (by storming off, throwing the board, tossing away the ball, or performing any other negative behavior), I'd strongly suggest you give your child a consequence for being a bad sport. An appropriate consequence might be saying, "You need to say you are sorry to the person with whom you were playing, and you can't play any winner-loser-type games/activities/sports for two days; then we get to try again."

#11: WHY ARE YOU CHEATING?
(OR: WHY ARE YOU BREAKING THE RULES? WHY ARE YOU LYING?)

Elliot and Diana shared that they have to be referees from the moment Tucker (age 5½) and Isabel (age 7) wake up until their heads hit the pillow every night. "They're constantly accusing each other of cheating, lying, stealing, and breaking the rules," declared Elliot, exasperated. "What's more, they sometimes question us about lying or rule-breaking too. We have to be on our toes all the time, to make sure we're not doing anything wrong."

When I asked for an example, Diana gave me several. "When Isie saw me pulling the car into a 'no parking' zone to wait for Elliot at the train station, she became distressed. 'Why are you breaking the rules? You're going to get into trouble…' and when Tucker thinks that Isabel has looked at his cards during a game, he'll start screaming, 'Why are you looking at my cards? That's cheating.' Then she'll yell back, 'I'm not! Why are *you* lying?' And every day one of them comes home from school with a story about how someone was unfair, lied, or broke a rule."

So what does it mean that your child is so concerned about the rules, especially when it affects the way he interacts with you, siblings, and people in the rest of his world? How do you respond to this question and others like it, to help your child behave in a socially appropriate manner?

Uncovering the Meaning

The beginning of school and a larger social life introduces a completely new dimension into the world of a young child. School is all about sharing, taking turns, telling the truth, and following rules. The school experience invites a child to explore the rules of fairness and honesty in a manner never expected of him before now. This is a good thing!

Developmentally, a child in this age range also naturally worries a great deal about what happens when one break the rules. He typically has great respect for those in authority: teachers, principals, police officers, and other authority figures. It is important for you to support this feeling during your child's early elementary years.

However, the concepts he is learning are all new to him, and he takes them literally. In addition, a young child has not yet learned to think in "grays." He thinks about his world in a very rigid, "black and white" way. Therefore, a preschool- or early-elementary-age child has a heightened sense of fairness, and of right and wrong. By this stage of development, he doesn't like cheating, which is why it is important for you not to tolerate it either, and he wants everyone to play by the rules—including you.

As part of his somewhat rigid thinking, he often only sees his own point of view as the right way and all others as wrong. This inflexibility gets him into trouble and causes him to sound accusatory, critical, and negative toward others. It is your job to help him learn to recognize that the way one speaks to others is an important part of building and maintaining relationships. Try to hold onto the skills you learn now, because when your child becomes a teenager, you will once again need them. Teens are not unlike children this age—they too only see their own points of view and will think that their parents are wrong all the time!

The Best Way to Respond

You will need to help your child begin to recognize that his personal black and white view may not be the only way to see the situation, and that asking his question in this way is likely to frustrate or anger the person whom he is asking. Each time you hear your child ask an accusatory question, your goal is to stop him before anyone gets a chance to respond (or before you respond yourself), and insist that he rephrase it in a less inflammatory way, for example:

- "Why are you cheating?" could become "I think you looked at my cards. If you did, could you please not do it again? If you didn't, don't worry about it."
- "Why are you lying?" could become "It makes me upset when I think you're not telling me the truth."

- "Why are you looking at my cards? That's cheating!" could become "Tucker, could you please try not to look at my cards, or tell me if I don't hold them up high enough?"
- "Why are you breaking the rules?" could become "Mommy, is it okay for you to park in this spot?"

It may not be easy for your child to make these changes or for you to insist on it, but it's far better to insist on it now while your child is young—and keep working on it for as long as possible. It will be worth it, because the more you practice it, the less argumentative and accusatory your child will be.

In addition, the more you work on this with your child, the more he will begin to learn that most situations are not black and white. This is a lesson that takes many years to perfect, but unless you begin teaching it now, your child may never learn it and could become one of those stubborn, insistent, "always needs to be right" adults with whom it is difficult to have a conversation. Remember, this black and white issue will most likely flare up again during adolescence, but if you have laid the groundwork in helping your child now to learn that there is always more than one way to see a situation, and if you keep reinforcing this all through his childhood, he will definitely be better equipped to enter adolescence and adulthood in a more mature, flexible manner.

#12: CAN YOU DRIVE ME TO SCHOOL?

"Courtney (age 7) asks to be driven to school every day," explains her dad, Nick. "I don't really mind driving her because it's on the way to my office. But shouldn't she be learning to get on the bus with the other kids? She says she likes being with me in the morning because she doesn't see me all day. But I'm not sure."

Children young and old ask this question, for a myriad of reasons. But when a really young child wants to be driven to school, the probable reasons are actually fairly limited. It's up to you to figure out why, so you can respond in a way that will be most emotionally beneficial for your child.

Uncovering the Meaning

There are a few different reasons that a young child doesn't want to get on the bus, so we'll explore them all so you can figure out which one best fits your child.

For a child who still struggles with separation issues, transitioning from being driven to school to taking the bus—even a small bus—can definitely trigger separation anxiety. Unlike being dropped off at the classroom, where her teacher is there to comfort and transition her, or even at the door to the school, where she knows she will be in her class within a minute or two, the loud, busy, and impersonal bus can be a challenge. She is forced to wave good-bye to you abruptly, often with other children watching as she tries not to cry. Then she has to watch you get smaller and smaller (perhaps waving sadly to her because you are not managing your separation too well either) as she holds in her feelings so the older kids on the bus won't make fun of her.

Another child who might ask to be driven to school is one that is more sensitive than other children are to loud noise. School buses are typically *very* noisy, and if your child becomes easily overwhelmed by this, it would not be surprising if she regularly asks you to drive her to school. Ask yourself the following questions to help you decide. If you answer yes to even one or two of the following questions, your child might be sensitive to loud noise:

- At big birthday parties, does your child remain on the outskirts?
- Does your child prefer watching movies at home, rather than at a movie theater (because it's loud)?
- Does your child cover her ears when she hears loud noises (sirens, banging)?
- Does your child resist loud music?
- At boisterous family gatherings, does your child tend to retreat to a quieter room?
- Does your child dislike indoor pools (because they echo loudly)?
- Does your child's teacher report that your child prefers quieter activities rather than noisy ones? (Ask the teacher.)

Your child might ask you to drive her to school if you have set the precedent, even if there is no specific reason for it. For example, perhaps you drove your child to school a couple of times at the beginning of the year, but now you don't want to do it anymore. On the other hand, maybe you were running late and your child missed the bus once or twice. And now, your child has come to expect it. She asks…asks again…cries a bit… so you give in and drive her. That's it; the pattern has been established.

One other reason that you may drive your child to school is peer pressure—all the other parents in your neighborhood drive their children to school, so your child is asking to be driven too—and you're feeling the pressure to be a "good parent" and drive yours as well.

Which is your reason? And what should your response be to the question?

The Best Way to Respond

In most cases, it is best to tell your child that she needs to take the bus to school. She needs to learn how to master the experience of separating from you, as well as negotiate the social experience and ability to be independent from you, that is a part of learning to be on the bus.

If you have previously driven her (set the precedent), explain that from now on she will be taking the bus. It is then up to you to make sure that the mornings run smoothly so that she gets to the bus on time. The more rushed you are, the more stressful it will be for her—particularly if she's anxious already. You may need to wake your child up—and of course yourself—a few minutes earlier in the morning. In addition, laying out clothes the night before, establishing a set routine (see Chapter Three, Question #13, for some ideas), and disallowing TV and computer before school, can all help immensely to make sure you have a calmer, less rushed morning. This will make getting to the bus stop easier. In addition, if you get to the bus stop with a few minutes to spare, it will probably be more fun for your child because there will be a few minutes to hang out with the other kids who are waiting for the bus.

If she has separation issues, make sure you leave enough time at home for your big hug and kiss. Then, at the bus stop, you should have a smile on your face the whole time—even if you have to fake it. Remind her that she will be fine and that you have confidence in her. Your goal is to make your child feel confident that she can manage her feelings and her time on the bus. You *do not* need to burden her with your own feelings. If you are anxious or upset about her going on the bus, keep it to yourself. This is your issue that you need to work out privately, without your child's knowledge. Your child needs the opportunity to learn how to enjoy herself on the bus and feel a sense of independence and accomplishment.

If you believe your child has difficulty with the noise

level on the bus, give her an MP3 player (or CD player). Load it with the type of music she enjoys, and give her a pair of noise-canceling earphones, which reduce the level of background noise so your child won't be tempted to listen to the music so loud as to cause hearing damage. This will not only drown out the noise on the bus, it will give her a sense of control over this experience. Just remind her to zip it carefully into her backpack when exiting the bus so she doesn't lose it or have it stolen.

One exception to this suggestion is that if your child is extremely sensitive to loud noise (perhaps she's been diagnosed with difficulty modulating sensory input), you may need to drive her to and from school, as the bus experience may be too neurologically taxing for her, and might set her up for difficulties the rest of the day. If your child finds even listening to music to be too loud, but she has not been diagnosed with anything, I strongly suggest that you speak to her doctor to determine whether any type of evaluation is in order.

3

Setting Limits and Boundaries

Every parent likes to have a well-behaved child—a child who listens to you, and whose company you and other people enjoy. It's not that you want a little robot, but it's great to have a kid who no one finds obnoxious or annoying. When your child behaves well, it's less stressful for you and for your entire family. What you may not realize is that you don't get a child like this by accident. In fact, it takes a considerable amount of consistent parental effort, beginning when your child is young. However, you have my word that it's worth every ounce of energy you invest, because not only will your efforts result in a super kid, but by the time your child is grown up, he will be an even more fabulous young adult. And don't worry, children in the preschool and early elementary grades are still so young that even if you think that yours is already a bit bratty, you still have plenty of time to put things right.

To this end, you will be interested to know that the way you respond to particular types of questions will take you a long way toward ensuring that your child is well-behaved. The answers to the questions in this chapter all involve the way you set limits, teach boundaries, and create expectations for your child's behavior. Parents struggle daily with these questions, because they are not sure how to answer them in a way that will show their children that good behavior is a clear expectation.

How can simply answering a question ensure that your child will behave well? Let's check out the questions, and you'll see what I mean.

#13: CAN I STAY UP LATER?

"No matter what time it is, or how tired they are, Hudson and Tyler (both age 5½) ask every single night if they can stay up later—just a few more minutes. We usually say no, but if it's a night when one of us gets home late from work, and we want to spend a little time with them, we might say yes. Or if we're having trouble getting the baby to sleep, they end up staying up later because no one is putting them to sleep."

The twins' parents, Emily and Michael, are not alone—this was one of the most common questions I received, and I heard it from parents of children not only in the pre-kindergarten to second grade age group, but on all age ranges. This doesn't surprise me, because the battle over who's in charge of your child's sleep—you or him—begins practically at birth and doesn't end until he's sleeping permanently under another roof. It's not always an easy battle, and when your child is older, I may suggest that he needs to begin taking charge of his own sleep schedule. But in these young years, I strongly recommend that you remain in control.

Uncovering the Meaning

Young children—all children in fact—love to test the limits their parents set for them. As tedious as this may be for you, challenging a parent is one of the primary ways a child learns which behaviors are acceptable and which are not. Each time you say no to your child, you communicate your disapproval of his request, and he knows that this is a clear boundary. Each time you say yes, you let your child know you approve of his request. This is true even if you don't really want to say yes but do so anyway because he's worn you down, because you don't feel like having an argument with him, or because you don't want to be the bad guy.

This concept is so important that it bears repeating:

> *Say* yes *to your child only when it is in his*
> *best interest, because when you say* yes, *he will*
> *assume it is because you approve of his request,*
> *even if you really don't.*

When it comes to bedtime, many parents allow their kids to stay up later—either by saying yes, or, like Emily and Michael when they're having a crazy night, by implying yes by not saying anything. When you do this, the message your child receives is, "If I ask every single night, then at least some of the nights I'll be a winner"—sort of like playing the slot machine.

By not having a clear and enforced expectation for bedtime, you give your child the message that he is more in charge than you are. This may be the path of least resistance, especially if you are juggling several children or a complicated life. However, *it is not in your child's best interest to have a chaotic or erratic nighttime schedule.*

Children in this age range need ten to twelve hours of sleep a night, and most are early risers, so you do the math! Each half-hour you let your child stay up later is enough to make him tired the next day. Sleep-deprived children do not do as well in school, they have a harder time socially and in sports, and they are more prone to a host of physical and emotional difficulties, including tantrums, depression, anxiety, and weight gain. By giving in to your child's request to stay up later, you are sending him the message that you would rather avoid his disappointment or anger than do what's best for his physical and emotional health. This is a message that will come back to haunt you again and again if you don't embrace it right now. One day your teenager might be testing your parenting limits by experimenting with alcohol or drugs. If you haven't taught him that you have clear expectations for his behavior by then, it will be exceedingly difficult to start at that point.

The Best Way to Respond

As you can probably see from our discussion so far, this is a question that will be much simpler to answer if you do some of the work beforehand. In fact, this work is an important part of creating behavioral expectations for your child.

Start by establishing a bedtime routine that begins after dinner that includes

- no more electronics (TV, computer, handheld games) at least thirty minutes (preferably one hour) before bed; electronics are stimulating (the lights, the activity), even if it seems that your child is calm while watching or playing, and they make it hard for your child to wind down.
- taking a bath
- brushing teeth
- putting on PJs
- reading a book
- getting into bed
- *going to sleep at the same time every night*

Once you have established this routine, and begun to stick to it, you will find that your child will not have the need to ask you this question nearly as frequently because he will know that your answer will practically always be no.

During infancy and toddlerhood, you can usually be more flexible with a child's sleep schedule, but by this age, the time that your child goes to bed should basically remain the same, regardless of whether you are working late, the baby is crying, or any other distraction. He needs to know that you care enough about his health to make this a priority. He has to wake up for school and be alert for learning, activities, and social interactions. This means you will need to invest the necessary time and effort to make sure this occurs. Following are four tips to ensure this:

- Keep a visual reminder of the routine on hand (laminated pictures on a piece of poster board work great at this age—your child can help create it).

- If you are not home, ensure competent child care, and reinforce that bedtime is important. It is particularly important to make sure that a grandparent is not secretly "making a deal" with your child to let him stay up later without telling you, in order to win favor in the eyes of your child. This will seriously undermine your parenting.

- Start the evening routine early enough that it can be completed by the established bedtime.

- Only say yes on *very* special occasions and on weekends. Even here, don't deviate from bedtime by more than an hour or so if at all possible. You can throw off your child's sleeping schedule for the week by changing it over the weekend.

#14: WHY DO I NEED TO TAKE A BATH? I TOOK ONE YESTERDAY.

Destiny, the mother of Chantal (age 4½), is thoroughly exasperated. "Chantal spends so much time arguing with me about whether she needs to take a bath that she could have been in and out of the tub in the same amount of time. And what really drives me crazy is that once she's in, she doesn't want to get out!"

I can't help chuckling when I consider Destiny's plight, as I've experienced it myself many times with my own children. They so resist the idea of getting clean, but somehow, once in, the warm, soapy water seduces them, and getting them out is equally difficult. So what's it all about?

For many young children, the frequency with which they take baths or showers seems to correlate very little—or not at all—with whether they are dirty. Rather, they typically see it as a waste of their precious time. A child views trying to get out of bathing as another parental boundary to challenge.

Uncovering the Meaning

Feeling a sense of autonomy over one's body is important for individuals of every age. However, realistically, young children have very few arenas over which they can experience personal autonomy. The first sense of physical autonomy a child experiences is at between two and about four years of age, through learning to master toileting. For some children and parents, this inadvertently becomes a battle when a parent wants the child to use the potty before she is ready or willing, and she refuses—thereby exercising control over her body in a different way.

Learning and practicing the skills of daily living—bathing, brushing teeth and hair—are the next way a child can exercise control over her body. Like toileting, if you take too much of this control away from your child, she will push back with a negative response—in this case by refusing to bathe or by giving you a big argument about it every time. However, if you don't have any expectations, your child will not properly learn these skills of daily living—crucial to growing up healthily, and not an area in which you should compromise as a parent.

So, how should you respond to this question with just the right balance?

The Best Way to Respond

Sometimes it is okay to skip a night. I bet you didn't think I'd say *that*, did you?

In order to give your child a sense of autonomy over her body and a chance to begin learning how to make decisions, it is a good idea to develop criteria for when she must take a bath or shower and when it is okay to skip a night. These rules will also teach your child that there are actual hygienic reasons for why she must bathe.

Create rules for your child. Try to create no more than three or four. Here are my suggestions:

- You can't skip more than one night in a row.
- You need to bathe if you've been playing outside, playing sports, or if you are sweaty, even if it's not "officially" a bath night.
- It is okay to skip if you've been inside all day and you didn't do anything dirty or messy, but you must wash your hands and face before bed.
- Some nights it is fine to wash your body, but not your hair. (This is an especially good rule if your child dislikes washing her hair or is afraid of getting shampoo in her eyes. In addition, this rule makes bath time a much more autonomous experience for many children who are able to wash their own bodies, but have not yet mastered washing their own hair.)

In addition, give your child a degree of autonomy over how much time she spends in the bath or shower. While there will be exceptions, do your best to allow her to bathe without rushing. If she can choose when to get out, you will get less resistance. If she really likes to linger, set a timer for about twenty minutes (or longer if it works for you), and tell her she can stay in until the timer goes off or get out any time before that.

Last, by preschool age your child is capable of washing her own body and often her hair—or part of it. For example, perhaps she can shampoo, but not rinse. No child is typically so filthy that she can't do an adequate job by now. Perfection is not necessary, but autonomy is essential. It is important that she learn to feel competent in this area. The same is true for teeth brushing and face washing. If you feel compelled to do everything for your child, she will not learn to do it for herself, nor will she believe you think she can do it for herself. Your child will fight you much less about bathing if you allow her the freedom to do it herself. Then stand back, and shower her with praise.

- -

#15: CAN I WATCH TV/USE THE COMPUTER/PLAY VIDEO GAMES FOR FIVE MORE MINUTES?
(TYPICALLY ASKED AFTER YOU HAVE ALREADY REQUESTED SEVERAL TIMES THAT THE TV/COMPUTER/VIDEO GAME BE TURNED OFF)

- -

No matter how many times Elizabeth asks her children to turn off the TV, Shawn (age 6), Brady (age 8), and Haylee (age 10) always ask her for a few more minutes. "It doesn't matter if the show is over, or even if it's a rerun they've seen ten times before. They always ask for 'five more minutes,' which inevitably turns into much longer. I feel like the TV rules our home!"

Does this sound familiar? Probably, because children

become "hooked" on TV, videos, and computer games beginning as young as two years old. These are incredibly engaging and are an easy panacea for parents when we need a break. There is also an educational value if we select carefully. But sometimes enough is enough! Why don't our children get the message?

Uncovering the Meaning

The reason for this question is clear. Like the others in this chapter, it is your child's way of testing one of the boundaries you have established. The way you respond to the question is important because it represents another opportunity for you enforce or reinforce good rules with your child.

In many families the TV (or computer or video console) does rule. In such a family, a child will treat this question more like a statement, because he knows his parent won't say no, or even if she does, the time for the TV to be turned off will come and go with no follow-through. In these families, there are so few rules about electronics that kids spend many more hours engaged with electronics than can be considered healthy for a child.

In other families, it is a little more erratic, because parents attempt to enforce a rule that they have established, but don't do so with any consistency. The mechanism by which this works is very similar to "Can I stay up later?" If you are not consistent in your response, your child will have little motivation to stop asking the question. In fact, the less consistent you are, the more likely he is to keep asking.

Here's an interesting psychological phenomenon that explains why:

Research on intermittent reinforcement, which is a part of the operant conditioning theory of the very famous psychologist B. F. Skinner (1904–1990), revealed that when you reinforce a behavior only some of the time (intermittently), it is even more difficult to eliminate that behavior than when you reinforce it all the time. It is the "slot machine" theory again, and it makes sense! Since your child never knows when you're going to say yes to "Five more minutes?" he keeps on asking—in fact, he often escalates the frequency of times he asks, hoping for you to say yes.

I bet by now you're already getting the hang of this, and that you can already anticipate how I am going to suggest that you respond to this question.

The Best Way to Respond
Now that you understand the reason for this question, responding to it should be clear. Begin by creating rules for all the electronics in your home. My recommendations are as follows:

- A *maximum* of two hours (I prefer one hour) of combined electronics per day—this means no more than the maximum of any combination of TV, computer, video games, handheld electronics, and any I may have left out. You can add one more hour for weekend days if you like.

- All homework, activities, playing outdoors, chores, and other responsibilities should be completed before electronics are permitted.
- Establish a way to keep track of how much time your child spends watching TV or using electronics. For example, don't allow the TV to be turned on all day and evening. Rather, decide with your child which shows he's going to watch. Then turn the TV on only for those shows. If your child is an electronics junkie, lock up the remotes or put a password on the computer so he can't have access to them at will. A kitchen timer works well for keeping track of computer and video game time for this age group.
- No matter how well you plan, a child this age still needs a couple of warnings when his time watching TV or playing on the computer or a video game is almost up. Unless your child has significant difficulty with transitions, a ten- and then a five-minute warning is typically enough.
- As always, make sure that childcare providers are clear about the new rules, and willing and able to support you in enforcing them.

Now that you have established boundaries, responding to the question will be easy. When you say, "Time is up," and your child asks you for "five more minutes," your response needs to be, "NO!" Remember the intermittent reinforcement theory—if you respond yes *some of the time,* you will be met with begging, pleading, and possibly tantrums *every time.* If you stick with no, you may still get asked, but it is very unlikely that you will get a real argument.

Setting clear boundaries on this issue during this stage of development is critical because as your child gets older and his interest in electronics becomes more diverse (for example, beginning to use the Internet), you will already be in a position to set effective limits. Believe me when I say that when your child is older, you will greatly appreciate having set these baseline rules during these early elementary years.

#16: CAN I HAVE ANOTHER PIECE OF CANDY?
(OR: CAN I HAVE ANOTHER COOKIE?)

You might think that this question should be in the "Nag, Nag, Nag" chapter, which is where I considered putting it. However, the truth is that setting limits around food (especially junk food), is one of the most important areas to face off with your child.

Sandra offers her daughters Olivia (age 8) and Madison (age 4) one junk food snack a day, but it doesn't seem to be working. "The girls get to choose one cookie or one piece of candy each day, but after they eat it, they always ask for another one. They don't stop asking until I finally give in and let them have a second. I always tell them that this is the last, but they beg and plead so sweetly that it's hard to say no. Also, I want everything to be peaceful in the evening when I come home from work, so sometimes it's just easier to give in and say yes. Is that such a big deal?"

Uncovering the Meaning

Kids love sweets! So it's understandable that your child will push this limit and ask for more each and every time. Of course, there are other reasons she might be doing so. If you have been reading this chapter carefully, you're already an expert on how your inconsistent behavior may be making your child push this boundary. If you are like Sandra, perhaps you make a rule (one piece of candy), but don't stick to it. Or perhaps you don't have clear-cut rules about food.

It is also possible that even at this young age your child is beginning to use eating to soothe emotional distress or to replace feelings of boredom. You are probably aware that the United States—and in fact most of the Western world—is fighting a serious battle against childhood obesity. Is your child on track to become one of the victims?

Childhood obesity can begin as young as two years old! It begins when a parent struggles to say no to a child when she asks for another piece of candy, a cookie, a handful of chips, or even a third helping of food. When you don't limit junk food or overeating by saying no, you give your child the message that her health is less important than having a temporary argument with her.

There are many reasons that parents don't set good limits around food. Ask yourself how many of these nine categories apply to you:

- You feel guilty saying no to your child.
- You work all day and want the evening to run smoothly, so you don't want to say no and have an argument.
- Food cheers her up when she is sad, disappointed, or angry. It's a quick fix that you would rather not give up.
- You figure you will deal with the consequences of unhealthy eating (weight gain, cavities, bad habits) when your child is older.
- You don't want to deprive your child of foods she likes.
- Money is tight and you often say no about big ticket items, so you want to say yes to something you can afford—junk food and second helpings are an easy yes.
- You never really thought about it before now.
- Eating brings a smile to your child's face, so why deprive her?
- The nagging drives you crazy, so you just give in.

So, how many are a yes for you? Even if it is only one, it's enough to make your child unhealthy. Next, we will discuss how to respond to this question, but if you think that your child may already be showing signs of being chubby or overweight, pick up a copy of my book *Dr. Susan's Fit and Fun Family Action Plan*. It will teach you *everything* you need to know about getting your child and your family on the road to good health.

The Best Way to Respond

Begin by setting a clear limit for your child. For example, when you hand her the first cookie, say, "You can have one; please *do not* ask me for any more because I will say no." When she asks for another cookie anyway, say a variation of the following: "I said you could only have one, and I meant it. The answer is still no, and if you ask again you will not get a cookie tomorrow."

I have said this throughout the chapter, but I will once again repeat it here. It is *most* important that you be consistent, clear, and keep your child's best interests—her health—in mind. There is no reason to be afraid of hurting your child's feelings, or worry that you are ruining the evening or depriving her of something. Saying no is a critical part of good parenting, even if you only have a couple of hours in the evening to do it. *Your child does not have to like you all the time.* This is not a gauge of whether you are a good parent—in fact, it might even mean the opposite. Often, being a good parent means upsetting your child or making her angry.

In addition, substituting food for money or material items does not show your child you love her. What's more, junk food is very expensive, so cutting down will save you money. Purchase only what you can afford, and teach your child the value of money.

If your child is sad, disappointed, or even bored, confront her feelings directly and help her cope with them—a hug, reassurance, and a few words are much more effective, and healthier than food.

Last, you must confront your child's health now. If you wait until later, it might be too late. More and more overweight children are developing adult-onset diabetes as preteens or teenagers. Even if your child shows no signs of ever being overweight, it isn't healthy to eat too much junk food. Begin teaching your child healthy eating habits now, and it will last a lifetime.

My bottom line: say no to requests for another piece of candy or a second cookie. Your child's body will thank you for it!

#17: WILL YOU COME HERE NOW?
(SOMETIMES YELLED!)

"When Nathan (age 6) wants something, he screams for me wherever he happens to be," reports Nathan's frustrated mom, Madeline, "and if I don't drop what I'm doing right away, he gets upset. Obviously, in 'Nathan world,' whatever he's doing is much more important than what I'm doing!"

Madeline is not the only parent of a pre-kindergarten to second-grade child who feels her young child is overly demanding and self-centered. In fact, a great many parents submitted similar versions of this question.

Uncovering the Meaning

Madeline's description of Nathan's behavior is accurate, because young children do often act as if their own needs are the only ones that exist. When your child was an infant and toddler, being completely self-centered was a natural part of development. A very young child is not able to see the world from any viewpoint but his own. He cries to have his needs met and does not have the cognitive ability to focus on the needs of others. It is impossible to rationalize with an infant, although toddlers certainly begin to understand the meaning of no.

As a child moves into the preschool and early elementary years, he begins developing the ability to recognize that, like him, other people have needs, interests, and desires. At this stage, your child is able to shift from being self-centered to being more thoughtful of the needs of others. However, just because he is capable of making the shift, it does not mean he will do so naturally. In fact, it is much more convenient for a young child to remain self-centered and "me" focused. Sometimes parents continue to indulge this behavior because they think it is cute, or because they believe their children will naturally outgrow it. This is most common with parents of only children or youngest children, because they are the most tolerant of less mature, more self-indulgent behavior. But it can be true of any parent and any child. Guess what? It is definitely not in your child's best interest to behave in a self-centered or demanding manner, and it is up to you to teach him to make the shift to being less so.

The way you respond to this question and others like it will go a long way toward teaching your child how to be less demanding, more polite, and less self-centered.

The Best Way to Respond

Of course, you need to first confirm that your child is not calling you to help him with a true emergency! Needless to say, in this instance, you should help him immediately. In all other cases, you should respond to your child in one of two ways:

- Go to where your child is, and say a variation of the following: "Stop yelling, because it won't make me do what you want. Tell me quietly with words, making sure you say 'Please.' When I am finished what I was doing, I will come back and help you. If you yell again, I won't come back and help you."
- Ignore his demand until he comes looking for you.

When he finally does come to you, explain that you don't like being yelled at, (especially if there was no "please" in the demand). Explain that you are in the middle of doing something (even if you are not), and that you can't stop doing it simply because he is yelling for you. Tell him that next time he wants you, he needs to come to where you are and ask politely for what he needs.

In both cases, role-play "asking politely" with your child (without yelling or demanding) for what he wants. When he slips up, be consistent about not giving in to his being demanding or rude to you. If you begin now, you will have a much more polite, less bratty child, as he grows up. It will not only be you who will benefit from this, but all the other adults in his life as well.

#18: WHY ARE YOU THE BOSS OF ME?

Manuel and Natalie's youngest daughter Maribelle (age 6½) is proving to be more of a challenge than her two older siblings have been so far. "Maribelle does not like being told what to do," reports Natalie, shaking her head.

"In fact," adds Manuel, "when it comes to doing something she doesn't like, she almost always demands to know, 'Why are you the boss? Why can't I be in charge of what I do?' How can such a little girl be so stubborn?"

If you are nodding your head in agreement because this sounds like your child, it's because many young children are like Maribelle! Your child simply does not like the idea of an adult being in charge of her, and she can't believe that you won't let her make all her own decisions about her life. Isn't it interesting how similar little kids are to teenagers?

In some cases a parent is worn down completely by the constant arguing and gives in every time, while in others she may stand firm each and every time. Which is better for your child? Is either the best way?

Uncovering the Meaning

As a young child begins exploring her world away from home, her self-confidence flourishes, sometimes with no bounds. For this child, confidence becomes a desire to control every element of her world. What's more, she convinces herself that she really does know everything! This results in her becoming upset and angry when a parent dares to exert any kind of appropriate control—setting boundaries and limits—in her life.

Other young children develop the desire to control because they have experienced significant upheaval in their lives. Being able to feel like they are in control of their everyday lives gives them a sense of security. This may be the case when a young child has experienced divorce, the death of a close relative, the birth of a sibling, or even a move to a new home.

As a parent, it can be exhausting to have a bossy, controlling child who doesn't want to let you make any decisions without a fight.

The Best Way to Respond

When you have a bossy child who doesn't want you to be in control of any aspect of her life, it won't help you to give in completely, nor will it be beneficial to stand firm each time on every issue. In fact, in order to develop a harmonious relationship with your child around this issue, you will find it most useful to let your child feel like the boss in some areas of her life, while you maintain control in the areas you deem most important.

My sister-in-law, Karen Silver, a truly talented elementary school teacher and the mother of twins Chloe and Hannah (age 7), has experienced this issue both professionally and personally. Chloe, who is very mature and self-reflective for seven, admits to being bossy! Chloe and Karen work hard to make sure that Chloe is able to "be the boss" of some aspects of her life. For example, in their home, Chloe is in charge of the girls' school lunch menu, and she makes her own lunch (and sometimes even Hannah's). Recently, Karen allowed Chloe to rearrange all the important things in her bedroom (books, toys, dolls, stuffed animals) the way she wanted, including placing signs for where everything should go. In addition, Chloe has a huge reusable calendar on her wall that Karen helps her create each month. Chloe likes to fill in the details of each day so she always knows what is coming up. This too gives her a sense of control. On the other hand, the rule in their family is that if Chloe does not do what her mom asks, she loses TV time (a big deal to Chloe).

Karen knows when to compromise with Chloe and when to set clear limits. She is willing to let go of control in some areas in order to maintain it in others that are important. By being flexible, Karen role-models for Chloe that being a good boss sometimes means letting someone else be in control. It also teaches her the valuable life lessons of compromise and not always getting her own way.

When your child asks you this question, it is not useful to say, "Because I'm your parent, that's why I am the boss of you!" For a child who wants to be in control of her own life, this will feel distressing and make her even more likely to buck your authority.

Rather, respond by saying a variation of the following: "I'm not the boss of you, but there are some things that you need to do, even if you don't want to do them. But there are some things that you can be the boss of. Let's decide together what you'd like to be in charge of, so you can feel like the boss too." By using Karen's model for allowing your child to feel in control in as many areas of her life as possible, it will be easier for you to maintain control in the most important areas as we have discussed throughout the rest of this chapter.

4

"I'm Scared"

Believe it or not, fears are one of the prevailing hall-
marks of childhood. In fact, almost no child escapes them
completely. For some children they begin as young as two
years old, and for others they continue into the preteen
and, less commonly, the adolescent years. Some kids have
only fleeting worries about minor issues, while others
seem to have persistent, nagging concerns that they can't
seem to shake. Because fears touch practically all children
at one time or another, you should be comforted to know
that in most cases they are considered perfectly normal.

Of course there can be times when a child's fears fall
outside of the realm of expected childhood behavior. So
before we even begin to understand your child's questions
associated with fears, I'd like to give you the criteria for
fears that should probably raise a red flag for you as a

parent. If your child's fears fit one or more of the following categories, it is a good idea to speak to your child's doctor, a school counselor, or a child psychologist or other therapist specializing in the emotional needs of kids:

- Your child's fear is interfering with her ability to function in daily life partially or fully (for example, but not limited to the following: they make separation terribly difficult for her; they prevent her from falling asleep, or they wake her up during the night; she is distracted by them so much that her schoolwork or social life is suffering).

- Your child's fear has lasted for more than a few weeks, and no matter what you say or do, it has not remitted even a little and may be getting worse.

- It was not precipitated by anything you can pinpoint, or if it was, the fear has long outlived the precipitant.

- Your child's fear is causing stress for the whole family because it limits everyone's choices, behavior, and actions.

- You have a "gut feeling" that, compared to other kids, your child's fear is just not healthy.

NOTE: I am a huge believer that parents should follow their gut feelings in almost all situations. After all, who knows your child better than you? So don't ignore your instincts. I have experienced countless situations where parents have come to see me after being dismissed by doctors, teachers, counselors, and even other family members who didn't think there was anything wrong with their children, but the parents just knew something wasn't quite right. By respecting the parents' gut feelings and investigating further, I have found that in many of these situations the parents were correct, and I was able to diagnose subtle learning issues or emotional difficulties that needed to be addressed. This is important because the earlier you get help for your child, the better.

It is not unusual for fears, especially anticipatory fears (the "what ifs"), to surface for the very first time around the age of four or five years old, and parents are often surprised to see them suddenly appear in their formerly happy-go-lucky children. Of course, as I have said (and will keep reminding you), child development is a range, so you may see your child's first fear at a younger or older age—or, in a few lucky cases, it may never appear. One of the main reasons fears develop now has to do with a child's realization that the world is not as perfect as she once believed. As a child develops cognitively and at the same time begins to separate from you (the parent who has protected her from the "big bad world"), the rose-colored glasses come off and she begins to see that sad and scary things can happen. Often this realization is triggered by her first major separation, the beginning of school, or, for some children, switching from a small nurturing preschool to a larger, more bustling kindergarten.

As you can see, children this age are developmentally primed to begin experiencing fears: they are becoming more aware each day, and at the same time leaving the safety net of home. Sometimes other experiences will actually instigate your child's first fear—a grandparent dying, a negative experience with a baby-sitter or friend, or an impending first-time flight. Even the regular routines that have never been scary before might now seem scary to a child in this developmental stage—a stage that reflects a real struggle between dependence and independence (are you feeling like a psychologist yet?).

The most common fear-related questions that your child will ask during this period are directly reflective of this developmental phase. And of course the way you answer them will be important, because the right kind of answer will help your child to move through the phase in an emotionally healthy way, feeling safe, secure, and, of course, less fearful. The six questions below were submitted by many parents—in these and slightly different formats. They were, by far, the most commonly asked questions in this age group, so I'm sure you'll find your child's questions reflected here. Pay close attention to the "Uncovering the Meaning" sections for each question because I will give you an even deeper understanding of the developmental issues that your child is facing at this stage. Understanding your child's fears and how to manage them is very important because *unmanaged fears don't always go away*. They can grow bigger and take on a life of their own. But with good intervention, you can easily help your child to feel better and master his fears.

#19: IS IT GOING TO HURT?
(A SHOT/BLOOD DRAWN/THE DENTIST/ BAND AID REMOVAL/EAR PIERCING/GETTING STITCHES/TRYING A SPICY FOOD/CATCHING A FAST BALL)

One dad, Marc, told me that whenever he tries to reassure his son Sammy (age 7), Sammy always says, "Yes, it will hurt, Daddy. You're just saying that it won't because you don't want me to be scared." Marc also reports that his daughter Abbey (age 5) begins to frantically scream, "Is it going to hurt? Is it going to hurt?" before any type of medical intervention, whenever she sees the doctor. Abbey doesn't seem especially interested in an actual answer from her dad, which makes him wonder why she's asking—or rather screeching—the question in the first place.

This is a fascinating question because sometimes a child will ask it calmly and curiously about a topic about which he seems merely curious. At other times he's already hysterically crying or screaming it in sheer panic over and over again as the doctor is about to put the needle into his arm, and you're feeling mortified embarrassment at his behavior.

Of course, given the strong reaction of some kids to hearing that something will hurt, sometimes parents refrain from telling the truth when asked, because they don't want their children to freak out in anticipation of the pain. They explain that they would rather deal with the children's crying afterwards than have to cope with the stress of trying to calm them down beforehand. These parents believe that the *anticipatory anxiety*—a very handy psychological term that means worrying about something before it happens— is worse than the actual pain. Many parents also don't want to have to deal with collateral issues like an impatient doctor or nurse waiting to give the shot. On the other hand, some parents tell their children the full-blown truth about the pain that they may feel, because they believe that it is never good to lie to a child about anything.

So which is the right way to handle this question? In order to understand the best way to respond, it is first necessary to understand the question from your child's point of view.

Uncovering the Meaning

Research shows us that there is a correlation between the amount of pain a person experiences and how much control he has (or perceives he has) over that pain. It is for this reason that hospitalized post-surgical patients are given control over how much pain medication they receive by being able to self-administer it, simply by pushing a button connected to an IV (of course only a certain amount will dispense so you can't overdose yourself).

How is this relevant to your child's question about whether something will hurt? Actually it's very relevant. It stands to reason that young children, who have very little control in their lives simply by virtue of their age, will have heightened concern about how much pain they are going to experience at any given time. No one asks them if they want to get vaccinations, have their teeth cleaned, or get their blood drawn. They're not even sure whether they'll be able to dodge a super-fast ball thrown in their direction or whether they will be hit hard by the ball because they're unable to catch it. It's tough being a little kid! But being able to ask the question—sometimes over and over—is the one thing your child can control. So now, the way I am going to teach you to respond to this question will reflect your knowledge that your child's fear is not only about the anticipation of experiencing pain—which often is rarely as bad as he anticipates (remember the "it wasn't so bad after all" feeling your child often experiences once it's all over). It is also about having no control over experiencing the pain in the first place.

The Best Way to Respond

Let's begin with whether you should tell your child about pain in advance or not. This is a good way to think about it: if a child is old enough to ask the question, he is old enough to understand the answer. He is also old enough to grasp the concept of you having lied to him. For this reason, it is important to be honest. While it may be tempting to always tell your child that it won't hurt because you want to avoid any drama, the long-term consequence will be that your child will learn to distrust what you say and recognize that you do not speak with authenticity. This will be a difficult reputation from which to break free. Even as your child gets older, it could impact on your relationship with him in many other situations. For example, he may not trust whether you are being honest when you tell him he is smart, or that you like what he is wearing, or that you will be home when you say you will. *Being authentic with your child is important, even if it is more difficult.*

This does not mean that you should instill panic in your child. When asked, the answer depends on whether your child will have any control over the pain. In some cases your child can't control whether or not he is going to experience pain—getting vaccinations and finger pricks, having cavities filled, and having other medical procedures are medically necessary—and it's important for a child to know that having these is not his choice, regardless of whether they cause a small amount of temporary pain. There is no emotional benefit to letting your child escape a medically necessary childhood vaccine or other similar procedure because he is afraid of pain.

But not having control doesn't mean your child can't feel some perception of control. In this case your response needs to include two components—one that acknowledges truthfully what will happen, and the other, which will give your child a perceived sense of control over the situation:

1. Respond with honesty, without panic: "Yes, it will hurt a tiny bit, but I know you can definitely handle it! It will probably feel like a pinch on your arm."

2. Teach your child the following visualization technique to distract him. As with any skill, he will need to practice it a few times before he needs to use it for real. (Try it yourself—it really works!) Say the following: "I am going to teach you a special trick to help you actually feel less pain. Close your eyes, and picture yourself somewhere that you really love (the beach, the park, Grandma's house—it can be anywhere, but it must be the same place each time). Think about being there—the sounds, smells, tastes, feelings. Imagine that you are really there. Visualize this every time you are just about to experience something painful."

If your child really can have some actual control over the anticipated pain, it is important to let him know that when you answer his question. Removing a bandage is a perfect example. You can respond by saying, "Why don't you take it off yourself? That way you can decide how much it will hurt, and I bet it will hurt even less then." Taking yucky-tasting medicine is another example. Some children prefer gulping it down all at once, others prefer sipping it, and still others like it diluted with a little water. Your child can decide which she prefers, as long as she knows she needs to take all the medicine. Even a good pediatric dental hygienist will tell a child, "Raise your hand if you need a break, and we can stop for a minute."

The key to responding to this question is always giving your child an actual or a perceived sense of control. It will immediately diminish your child's anxiety and worry, while maintaining a truthful and reassuring relationship with your child.

#20: HAVE YOU TURNED ON THE ALARM?
(OR: CAN WE GET AN ALARM? HOW COME WE DON'T HAVE AN ALARM? ARE THE DOORS LOCKED? WHAT HAPPENS IF SOMEONE BREAKS IN?)

Wendi (age 6) asks her parents, Carol and Ed, this question every single night, almost as part of her bedtime routine. They don't understand why, because each night they offer the same answer—yes! Many kids are just like Wendi, and while others may not ask quite as often, they still display a heightened interest in making sure the house is secured at night and even when the family goes out. Clearly, simply responding yes (or no) does not work to make a young child feel secure, which is why she keeps asking. It is therefore important to understand a young child's need for security before responding to this question.

Uncovering the Meaning

As you now know from reading the beginning of this chapter, fears become more prevalent as your child moves into the preschool and the early elementary years. It therefore makes sense that the house alarm or locked doors and windows could take on an important role in a child's life. However, it is unlikely that this alone would make a child so focused on issues of home safety. It is likely that other factors would have to be added to feed this particular fear—ones that make your child feel that she needs to be protected in her home.

One common way for this fear to develop is when a young child is exposed to scary media. For example, sometimes without even realizing it, a parent may allow a child to watch or listen to the news or to TV shows that are frightening, or to see newspaper or magazine pictures or articles (if a child is beginning to read) that are scary. Even snippets of such media can terrify a child. She may develop difficulties falling asleep and certainly she will want to check and double-check that the alarm is activated or that the doors and windows are locked. Even older children—sometimes even teenagers—can be scared by the news.

In addition, you don't always have control over everything your child hears and sees. The bus and playground are rampant with shocking stories told by older children, especially designed to terrify the younger ones. This is a rite of passage for which you need to need to be prepared, especially if you have a child who is on the sensitive or gullible side.

Another trigger for a child's interest with home safety is hearing about a robbery or mugging in your neighborhood—it can evoke fears of one occurring in your home. Even hearing about or witnessing kids being bullied at the corner playground can cause a child to want extra protection. It is important not to dismiss or trivialize such a fear, especially if something real has happened to cause it.

Last, but by no means least, children take cues from their parents. If you display anxiety about setting the alarm, locking up your home, or your family's safety, or if you discuss fears or worries in general in your child's presence, your child is much more likely to become fearful about these things too. As a parent, it is your job to do your best to contain your own fears so you don't pass them on to your child.

Therefore, before we get to the best way to answer

this question, adhering to the following tips can help alleviate a nervous child's fears:

- Keep TV and radio stations (in the house and car) tuned to child-friendly stations while a young child is awake—even when you think she isn't listening or in the room. Make sure that older siblings and childcare providers also respect this rule (including grandparents).

- When your child tells you about her day at school, listen for stories that may be making her anxious— "tall tales" that sound silly to you but could be scary to her. Discuss them with her and alleviate any fears of them being real.

- Don't lie or pretend if your child has heard about something scary happening in the neighborhood. (We will discuss in the next section how to talk to your child in order to comfort her fears.) Remember, authenticity is important.

- Don't overreact, panic, or display fears or anxieties around your child—remember, you're the adult!

The Best Way to Respond

Some questions are best answered with a question—this is one of those questions. You will learn more about what is worrying your child and how truly to address it, if you respond with a variation of one of the following:

- "Are you worried?"
- "What are you worried about?"

- "What are you thinking about?"
- "What feelings will the alarm help you with?"

The answer to one of these questions should open a conversation with your child about her underlying concerns or fears. Listen closely for these and address them. In addition, your conversation should contain the following points:

- Her safety is your top priority.
- It isn't the alarm that keeps her safe at night. Rather, the adults in her life make choices and decisions to ensure her safety. This is an important point, because if the alarm should break or if she sleeps somewhere with no alarm you do not want her to feel unsafe. For example, she may sleep at a friend's home that doesn't have an alarm, but she should trust that you will let her sleep there because you've determined that it is safe—you can use this as an example with your child.
- Give her examples of other times that you make choices to ensure that she is safe (holding her hand to cross the street, being careful around the stove, not leaving her alone in stores). Explain that making sure she is safe at night is no different. Tell her she doesn't have to worry about the alarm each night—you're always thinking about her safety.
- One of your goals is to begin to break the cycle of her asking the question so that it does not become a

long-standing habit that feeds her fear. To accomplish this, tell her that each night when she thinks about asking you the question, she should instead tell herself, "I know Mommy/Daddy keep me safe all the time, so I don't have to ask."

- If this question persists or gets worse, making it difficult for your child to sleep at night, reread the red flags at the beginning of this chapter in case you need to get some extra support for your child to break the cycle.

#21: IS THERE A MONSTER/GHOST IN MY ROOM?

Unlike the question above, this question reflects your child's worries about potential threats (typically imaginary) inside your home—even inside his head. However, parents don't always know how to answer it. Marilyn, mom of Kyle (age 6), summarizes the dilemma well. "Part of me feels bad for Kyle when he tells me he's afraid of the Closet Monster. Part of me thinks that I should just tell him it's silly and he should get over the fear, and another part of me wants to tell him that if he would just keep his closet neater it wouldn't look like there were monsters living in it!"

Sometimes parents remove closet doors, take all the clothes from the closet, take off bed ruffles, and cast pretend magic spells to offer reassurance to their kids that they are safe from monsters during the night. Sometimes these work, but not usually. In fact, in most cases parents report that these techniques don't diminish the questions or fears at all, and may even escalate them.

Why do children have these types of fears, and what is the best way to manage them?

Uncovering the Meaning

I think Marilyn speaks for most parents. She feels sympathetic about her son's plight, but at the same time she wants to give him a dose of reality and she also experiences normal frustration that he won't easily go to sleep at the end of a long day.

As we have been discussing, beginning around nursery school age and continuing into the early elementary years, kids' imaginations are at their peak. We adults marvel at the fantastic games they play at home and in school, weaving fabulous stories for hours, alone or with friends. But it's this same creative force that comes to life at night, causing kids to imagine every possible kind of frightening monster and creepy ghoul, both before they fall asleep and during their dreams. It is not surprising, therefore, that this is such a common question. Your child's normal imagination gets away from him even more than usual when it is dark outside. Should you fight the imaginary monsters with him or dissuade him from their existence?

The Best Way to Respond

The answer is that you *should not* respond to his monsters by pretending they are real. By searching for monsters under the bed or in the closet, by taking down doors or bed ruffles, you will immediately send your child a clear message that there is something real of which he should be afraid—a monster that you need to find. So what will you do when you find this monster? You're not sure? Your child may be wondering too, especially since each night you look but never find the monster, which means it may still be hiding somewhere in his room. Sounds creepy, huh? Even a night light gives your child the signal that you too believe that he needs protection from the dark and whatever may lurk within it.

When your child asks you about monsters or ghosts, you should respond with a variation of the following: "There is nothing scary in your room or in our house. Sometimes you may have some scary thoughts; lots of kids do. But guess what? When you have a scary thought, you can think a happy thought instead, and it will make you feel better." Then help your child generate some pleasant thoughts to replace the scary ones that pop up. You can also teach your child the visualization technique we discussed earlier in this chapter. It can be very effective for erasing monsters!

If your child is especially afraid, and insists on you staying with him, or if you are already in the habit of lying down with your child for this or another reason, it's time to send your child the message that you trust his ability to use his own skills to take care of himself. Refer to Chapter Six, Question #29, for an excellent technique describing how to do this effectively. Explain that you know there are no monsters, and that you are only going to do this for a few days while he works with you on helping himself by thinking the happy thoughts instead of the scary ones.

#22: DOES IT HURT WHEN SOMEONE DIES?

Paula, mother of twins Amanda and Lindy (age 4½), told me that when Paula's mother died, the girls overheard a conversation among relatives about how good it was that their grandmother "hadn't suffered." They asked their mom what that meant, and she explained as best as she could to the four-year-olds. Paula says, "Ever since my mom died, the girls have been worried that some people *do* suffer when they die—and they worry that everyone in their own family, including themselves, might suffer. I'm not sure what to tell them. I feel like I accidentally opened a can of worms!"

It can be a painful and sad milestone for a parent to hear a child begin asking questions about death, because you realize that once she understands death, you can no longer protect her from the harsh realities of the world. Depending on a child's life experiences (a grandparent or a pet dying), this may begin as young as nursery school age. However, for most children, a meaningful grasp on the permanence of death does not begin until preschool or the early elementary years. Parents are typically ambivalent about how to answer this question, realizing that it can end in a quagmire of even more confusing questions.

Uncovering the Meaning

To begin, it is critical to recognize that in this age group, any question about death is a reflection of a child's personal fears and has *nothing* to do with a philosophical curiosity about death. You should *always* keep this in mind when responding to this or other questions about death.

As a child begins to mature cognitively and she becomes exposed to more life experiences in her family and social world, there is further opportunity for her to experience the concept of death. Perhaps in school she hears about the death of a peer or teacher's relative, learns to comfort a friend, and talks about death (of a pet or a person) with classmates. For children, discussion can be soothing and educational. It helps them to integrate a new life experience. It also forces them to think of questions and worries with which they may not previously have concerned themselves.

At different stages of development, children worry about various aspects of death. If you have a child at the older end of the range of this book, you may want to read *The Top 50 Questions Kids Ask (3rd through 5th Grade)*, to get an understanding of how this fear can change over time, because as you know, some children go through stages earlier and some do so later.

So what is the best way to respond when your child asks you this question? Honestly? Protectively?

The Best Way to Respond

Before answering this question, ask yourself whether anything has precipitated your child asking it. Do you have an ailing family member, friend, or pet? Has someone (or a pet) just died? If the answer is yes, it is best to first respond to this question by addressing this issue head-on. Rather than answering the question, say, "I'm wondering if you're thinking about [name of person/pet]." Then wait for an answer. If your child says yes, keep asking as many questions as you can before answering. For example, "Are you worried about [the person/pet]?" "Do you think they have pain?"

The more your child tells you, and the more dialogue you have, the better you will understand your child's fear. Furthermore, your child may actually feel better simply by voicing her concerns. If you can't uncover a reason for the question—despite trying—I have the following piece of advice.

Ask your child this question before offering any sort of answer: "Do *you* think it hurts when someone dies?"

In many cases, your child will offer a response that is more satisfying to herself (and even to you) than any you could possibly provide, no matter how hard you try. What she says is likely to comfort her and make her feel secure (for example, "No, I don't think it hurts, because when you die you don't feel anything."). Her response may not be *factually* accurate—in fact it may be incorrect—but it doesn't matter, as long as it soothes her. There will be plenty of time as she gets older to correct facts. When she provides you with a response that she considers satisfying, all you have to say is the following: "I think that is a great answer and I agree with you!"

In fact, this is true for a great many of the questions that your young child will ask you on tough topics. I challenge you to try it. Given the opportunity, in almost every case your child will ask and then answer her own questions in a way that will comfort her. All you will have to do is nod and agree.

If your child can't soothe herself because her anxiety is too great, you will, of course, need to step in with a response. This is also true if she is questioning information that she's learned about death (like Paula's twins above). It is not advisable to provide graphic information about death to a child in this age range because typically this will make her feel even more scared.

Your answer to this question should primarily be to offer comfort—even if it means fudging the truth a bit.

Any thoughts that death is painful could result in a child not only becoming terrified in anticipation of herself or others dying, but she might also become afraid of going to sleep at night, because many children don't yet understand the difference between sleep and death. Your response should sound something like the following: "When people die, they feel peaceful and calm. Their bodies stops working, sort of like how when a toy runs out of batteries, it stops working. Since their bodies don't work anymore, they don't feel any pain at all. Dying doesn't hurt, and it isn't scary. It isn't something that you need to be afraid of."

#23: ARE YOU MAD AT ME?

Miriam, mother to Jonah (age 5) and Noah (age 8), tells me that her children ask this question every single day. "It drives me crazy because they ask so often that sometimes I wonder if they are really worried or if it's just a habit!"

Other parents express that their children ask the question whenever a parent raises her voice, whether it is at the child or not. It seems to these parents that their children are confused, not knowing at whom their parents' anger is directed and always assuming it is directed at them—thereby precipitating the question.

Uncovering the Meaning

This is one of the most fascinating and powerful questions in the book because it doesn't just indicate a child's fear that his parent might be disapproving of his behavior; it also frequently reflects a feeling of guilt, which is a brand new emotion for young children. Your child may feel guilty if he did something he wasn't supposed to do. He may also experience misplaced guilt even if he did nothing wrong.

In addition, this question marks the beginning of a child's verbalized recognition that his behavior can have a direct impact on his parent's mood. In this regard, this question is related to Question #17, "Will you come here now?" from Chapter Three, because it too demonstrates that your child is beginning to become aware of his impact on other people's feelings and behavior. All that in one small question!

However, this question can also be a barometer for something else—*your own behavior*. Get ready, I'm about to teach you about another psychological term called *displacement*. When a child asks this question frequently, it is sometimes because his parent is often in an angry, bad, or irritated mood and is directing this mood toward, or taking out bad feelings on a child—perhaps without even realizing it. For example, if you have a bad day at work (or a fight with your mother) and then you yell at your child for something minor, your child is likely to believe that you are mad at *him*—that he did something bad. If you frequently *displace* your anger onto your child (by becoming angry with him for minor things when you are really upset about something else in your life), your child will start to internalize the feeling that you really disapprove of him, don't like him, or that he is the cause of your problems. Therefore, if your child is asking you this question all the time—at this age or any other, through adolescence—I strongly suggest that you begin by asking yourself the following questions:

- Do I yell more than once a day?
- Am I angry most days? Do I feel angry most of the time?
- Is it possible that I am displacing my anger/ unhappiness/disappointment by acting angrily with my child?

If you answered yes to any of these, I first congratulate you on being honest with yourself. Second, it is time to work toward becoming more aware of channeling your frustrations in healthier ways—take a walk, write, talk to a friend, learn some stress-relieving techniques, or seek professional help to make changes that will make you happier. You need to begin to do anything other than taking it out on your child.

If your child has actually behaved inappropriately, this question is simply a response to your expressed disapproval of the negative behavior. It is important to be sure that your discipline "fits the crime" and is not overly harsh. But assuming this to be the case, the question is his way of trying to open up communication in order to win you back over to his side again and diffuse the stress between you. Do not allow your anger or disapproval to get in the way of your being able to have a calm conversation with your child about his behavior. No matter how upset you may be, it is important not to allow your bad feelings to linger indefinitely.

The Best Way to Respond

Don't lie to your child by saying that you are not mad—it will be confusing for him because he can see that you look angry. If his behavior warranted your becoming angry, it is important for you to respond to this question by saying, "Yes, I am angry." But don't stop here. Follow with a very specific explanation of why you are angry: "You climbed on the table even though I've told you never to do that! And you broke the table and could have hurt yourself. That makes me very angry."

Last, always end with an affirmation that no matter how angry you are now, you will eventually stop feeling angry, and that even when you are angry you still love him: "Right now, I'm angry, but even when I'm angry I love you. In a little while I won't be angry anymore, but you will still have a consequence for jumping on the table and breaking it."

If you are not angry *with him*, ask him why he thinks you are angry. If he says you look or are acting mad, pay attention to it. Perhaps you are behaving in a way that is angry without even realizing it. Maybe it is time to change your behavior—as we discussed earlier. Acknowledge this to your child, and tell him you will work on it. He will be relieved to hear this.

5

Little Kids Can Be Spiritual

One of my all-time favorite activities is to eavesdrop on a group of five- or six-year-olds who are deep in debate about the spiritual world. We adults sometimes assume that at such a young age children are not yet pondering the puzzling notion of praying to God—a being you can't see, feel, or prove, but must somehow believe in completely if you so choose. This type of philosophical struggle, one would think, is part of the domain of adolescence. Children just beginning school generally take everything we tell them at face value and believe it, right?

During the preschool and elementary years—especially the early ones—kids are generally "rule followers." They love to know the face value of everything right up front. That is why young children love board games so much—so many rules! Even when they are cheating, they're practicing "breaking the rules" in a safe way—let's call this a dress rehearsal for the sometimes much bigger adolescent rule-breaking. For this reason, young children thrive best on routine, structure, and doing exactly what their parents tell them (more on the importance of rules and structure in Chapter Three). So one would expect a young child to simply accept it when we tell them that God exists (or doesn't, if that's what you believe) without too much fanfare.

But that's where you'd be wrong!

It is for this very reason that young children ask so many questions about God, religion, and spiritual life. In fact, you'll see as we begin to explore the top questions about God and spirituality, it's the very fact that *there are no observable rules that prove or govern God's existence* that make it difficult for your early-elementary-age child to simply take God's existence at face value. Hence the questions. Developmentally, it makes sense. The many questions you may be asked about God, the curiosity about what happens when someone or something dies, and even the struggle to understand how religion fits in with "regular" life—all of these are your child's way of trying to find a set of rules to explain and organize an otherwise vague and non-rule-governed arena. We won't discuss fear of death in this chapter—that's a different type of question that is addressed in Chapter Four (you can check back and reread it, if you don't remember).

Children this age do not yet have the cognitive ability to think philosophically or abstractly (no, not even your brilliant child!), and this ability does not begin to develop until the late elementary years, through middle school, and then it truly blossoms in the teen years. If you have an older elementary-age child, or if you have a copy of *The Top 50 Questions Kids Ask (3rd through 5th Grade)*, take note of the type of questions children in that age range are asking about God, religion, and spirituality. You will begin to notice an important shift, not only in the questions, but also in how you should be responding in order to help your child grow emotionally and cognitively!

The way you answer these kinds of questions now, in the early elementary years, should reflect your child's seedling struggle with the idea that not everything can be explained or understood "by the rules." Your responses should gradually begin to challenge your child to look at the world a little differently. At the same time, your responses should respect the idea that young children really need to be concrete in order to feel comfortable and safe in their world. As we go through the questions and answers you will see how these two areas are balanced.

The reason that "God and religion" questions are important—thereby deserving of a chapter in the book—is because they represent this struggle between the explainable and the unknowable. Over time, every child will have to come to terms with many things in life that cannot necessarily be explained or placed into a neat little box, physically or emotionally. It only just begins here.

This struggle will increase and deepen in intensity gradually over the next ten or twelve years as your child's cognitive skills mature and sharpen. So hold onto your seat! If you continue to successfully communicate with your child through all the challenges of his or her development, before you know it, you will be having deep philosophical discussions and perhaps even heated arguments with your sixteen-year-old about God and the universe.

To help you on your way to that great path of wide-open communication, let's get to the top questions about God, religion, and spirituality. Begin here with a solid base and each step afterwards will be that much easier—at least until the teen years. Then all bets are off!

- -

#24: WHERE IS GOD?

- -

Tom, a dad I spoke with, explained the dilemma of this question well: "When Larry asked, 'Do you know where God is, Dad?' I was stumped. To be honest with you, I'm not exactly sure myself!"

In fact, many people struggle with this very question even as adults, and when their young children approach them with it, it evokes a feeling of being unsure—even in those with a deep spiritual or religious conviction.

Your initial response might be very vague ("God is everywhere" or "God made the world a long time ago" or "God isn't a real thing") because you are unsure how to respond. On the other hand, you may try to give your child a complex, all-encompassing explanation in order to make sure you haven't left out any possibility ("God is in every flower, every ocean, and even in your breakfast cereal. God watches you in school and is there even when you sleep.")

The truth is, neither of these types of responses will satisfy your child's developmental reason for asking the question—the need for a concrete response. So, how do you answer this question, to which there really is no concrete answer?

Uncovering the Meaning

Since neither of the above responses is actually provable, either one is most likely to evoke a succession of other questions, because your child is still trying to get a concrete answer. The first, vague response will likely be met with "How can God be everywhere at the same time?" "Where did God go after he made the world?" or "Why do people pray to God if he isn't real?" Furthermore, some children become scared when you tell them that God is everywhere. It worries them that God can see them naked in the shower, using the bathroom, or even sleeping.

Your child might respond to the more complex answer with something like, "If God is with me all the time, when is he with all the other people?"—the cognitive concreteness of your young child is operating at full force! What's more, as you can see, for a child with a strong sense of responsibility, this response may even evoke a feeling of guilt: he feels bad that if God is with him, others are being deprived.

I'm sure you recall from the beginning of this chapter that children in the preschool and early elementary years need to understand the "rules of the game" in order for them to feel safe and satisfied. God—whom they can't see, feel, hear, or touch—certainly doesn't fit any rules to which they have been exposed up until this point in their lives. Therefore, if you answer the question either by being too vague or by giving too much information, your child will be confused, but most importantly, will not feel like the question has been adequately answered. In this case it is a *literal* question. At this age a child is actually asking, "Is God in the sky, here on earth, in the attic, hiding in that tree, in the ocean, or where exactly? I need to know exactly where I should be looking and what I should be looking for." In other words, "Could you please tell me the rules of this God hide-and-seek game so I can also play?"

There are several variants of this question that you may have heard from your child. Some of these are, "What color is God?" "Is God a boy or a girl?" (read more about this interesting question when you get to #27) "Is God bigger than the house?" Although these may sound like completely different questions, they are still your child's way of trying to make God fit into terms that are familiar within his world. For example, your child might be feeling something like, "If I know what color God is and if God is a boy or a girl, and if he is smaller than a tree, then I bet I can draw him with my crayons." This would be a comforting thought for a seven-year-old struggling with the notion of an abstract greater being. Or "If God is bigger than a house, then he (or she) might be easy to spot when I'm on my way to school tomorrow," is another reassuring feeling for a six-year-old trying to discover God.

The question or questions your child asks about where God is and what God looks like may feel frustrating to you. This is because they are so specific and because there is really no way you can actually answer them in the literal way that would satisfy your child right now, except by fabricating a response such as, "Yes, God is a very tall man with long black hair and bright blue eyes. He's probably wearing a flowing white shirt, khaki pants, and sandals. Keep an eye out for him!" While such a specific response might stop the questions for a little while, the truth is, before long your child will reach another stage of development and begin questioning you again. But, even before that, he will speak to other kids who will have heard different versions of where God may be and what God looks like, and your child will begin to question the specifics of your temporary, stop-gap explanation.

The Best Way to Respond

Keep in mind that your child is looking for a concrete answer, but at the same time recognize that no such response exists for this particular question. In situations such as this, it can be very useful to respond to the question with another question: "Where do you think God is?" By asking this question you will elicit your child's thoughts and feelings about God. If necessary, your question can be tweaked. For example you might ask, "What color do *you* imagine God is?" "Hmm, I wonder; do you think God is a girl or a boy?" or "What size do you think God is—bigger than a house, smaller than a tree, or even smaller or bigger than that? What do you think?"

By deflecting back to your child, you will give him the opportunity to formulate his own answer, which will be correct for him. You will simply need to affirm it with something like, "That sounds about right to me!" You can even continue to ask your child further questions in order to understand what he is imagining or thinking about God. For example, if he says, "I think God is a boy," you might ask, "What do you think he looks like?" or "How old a boy do you think he is?"

Of course, it is possible (although less likely) that your child will eventually insist that you give him the "right" answer. At that point, you need to respond by telling him a version of the following: "I agree with you. I think that you have a pretty good idea of where God is. But, if you like, we can talk about God again soon, in case our ideas change." This response gives your child the affirmation he needs while still showing him that this is not a subject for which there is a clear-cut answer.

#25: CAN GRANDMA/GRANDPA [WHO DIED] SEE US?

Like many parents, Rosemary told me that she always responds to this question with a teary, "Yes, of course Grandma can see us! Even though she can't be with us, she's watching us from above." However, she admitted to me, "It is sometimes difficult to know whether this type of absolutely definitive response is more comforting for me than for Jeremy (age 3) and Emily (age 5). I miss my mother—more than my kids do—and it makes me feel good to think that she's watching us from heaven."

Your child might be wondering how you know for sure that the deceased person could be seeing them—do you have a special knowledge about death that she doesn't yet possess, but eventually will when she grows up?

When thinking about this question, it is important to begin by separating *your feelings* from *your child's needs*. This can be tough to do when we are discussing a topic like death—because it really tugs on your heartstrings. But nonetheless, being a great parent means often having to put your child's needs first, right? This is one of those times.

Uncovering the Meaning

When young children ask this question it is usually because they are struggling with the concept of death and what actually happens to a person after dying. In this instance it is not so much about the fear of dying—fears usually provoke different types of questions (see Chapter Four). Rather, your child—who has a developmental need for concrete answers—literally wants to know if the departed person is still able to watch what is happening in the world of the living.

This question is sometimes the result of a child not yet fully grasping the meaning of death, possibly because a parent has found it too painful to explain death medically and has instead done so with euphemisms. For example, more than one preschooler or kindergartner has informed me that her grandparent has died and gone to the attic ("above"), where he or she is now living and watching over the family.

Of course, each parent has a different theory or spiritual/religious belief about what actually happens to the "spirit" of a person after he or she dies. This personal conviction can be woven into the response you give your child. However, it is still important to respond to this question keeping the following two points in mind:

1. Your child's opinion is of primary importance (as in Question #24).
2. You should not let your beliefs completely suppress your child's feelings.

The Best Way to Respond

As with Question #24, begin by responding with a question: "Do *you* think Grandma can see us?"

Then listen carefully to your child's answer, because it will tell you a great deal about your child's feelings and beliefs. Does she miss her grandparent? Is she sad? Is she worried that her grandparent is lonely, in pain? Maybe she is relieved that she is gone? Are there many other things that she believes her grandma is doing now that she is "gone"? Keep asking questions and allowing responses until you feel satisfied that you have a complete understanding of what your child really was wondering when she asked the initial question. I bet you will be surprised to find much more to her curiosity than if you had simply taken the question at face value.

Remember how we began this section: it is important to keep your own feelings in check. Even if you are discussing a death that is very sad for you, keep focused on your child's emotional needs and respond to them as concretely as possible in a way that will help your child feel emotionally secure. Your goal is to feel comfortable addressing her concerns beyond the initial question. So if she's worried that her deceased grandparent (or pet or whomever she's discussing) is lonely, hurt, or upset, it is fine to reassure her that after a person dies, the person doesn't feel pain or bad feelings. If she misses the person, suggest that she and you draw pictures, look at photos, or tell stories that will bring back good memories.

If she insists on a concrete answer to the specific question, it is best to make your response as comforting and non-frightening as possible. While this may be difficult to do and may even be counterintuitive if you have strong spiritual/religious beliefs, it is important to help your child through this period without feeling trauma about dying. Sometimes you need to withhold information in order to ensure this, keeping in mind that your child's emotional needs are of paramount importance. Perhaps she loved her grandmother, and it brings her solace to think that her grandma is watching over her. On the other hand, perhaps she didn't like her grandmother, and she'd prefer to believe that she is nowhere to be found.

Over several years of growing up, her beliefs about death are likely to change many times, but right now it will be most beneficial to allow her current ideas to lead the way. It will not be beneficial for you to force her to think and feel differently than she does right now about a topic for which there is no proof either way. Secondary to this will be to make sure that the information you share with her is innocuous, gentle, and not scary.

#26: DID GOD MAKE _____ [YOU NAME IT]?

I received this question in many different formats, ranging from long lists, to very specific items (flowers, clouds, schools, people, pets, toys). Courtney says that her son Thomas (age 4½) " is going through a phase when he asks this question a hundred times a week—a day— until it drives his dad and me crazy! We find that no matter how many times we answer the question about one thing—whether the answer is yes or no, Thomas will soon be asking if God made something else."

Many young children are just like Thomas. What is the best way to help your child understand the concept of what God creates vs. what people create? While it may not seem so on the surface, it is actually a complex issue for young children. But first, we need to tackle the all-important issue of what your child is *really* trying to understand in asking this question.

Uncovering the Meaning

As an adult, you likely have a fully evolved belief system about the role that God plays (or does not play) in your life. Your preschool- or early-elementary-age child has not yet had the opportunity, nor does he have the cognitive ability, to have formed a comprehensive, clear opinion about God's role in his world. I am *not* talking about evolution vs. creationism. Rather, I am discussing the question of whether—from a child's viewpoint—it is God that creates clouds, or it is the water cycle that creates them. Is it God that created the toy I love so much, or is it made by humans?

We're talking about *fact vs. faith.*

Your child is not sure yet which to believe—or whether both have a place in his life. His desire to test out the idea that a higher being is in charge of creating everything (faith) flies in the face of the developmental yearning to have provable, factual knowledge (examples: Mom made this PB&J sandwich, a science project proves the water cycle, I built this sand castle). Be aware that this curiosity about God may develop even if *you* don't believe in God.

In addition to curiosity, there is another developmental issue at play. For a young child, the need to be concrete fights an internal war with the superbly developed *ability to suspend his disbelief.* Being able to suspend one's disbelief is a psychological term (I told you you'd become an armchair psychologist!), which means that even in the face of stark reality, a person can convince him- or herself that the complete opposite is true. This is why young children are able to truly believe in Santa Claus, the Tooth Fairy, and the Easter Bunny. When you read *The Top 50 Questions Kids Ask (3rd through 5th Grade)*, you will see that these beliefs become the subject of a prevalent question for older children, who are developmentally much less able or willing to suspend their disbelief.

Your child's persistent questions to qualify what God does and doesn't make (even if you feel that you have answered this question multiple times) can be the result of his attempt to convince himself that God makes everything, regardless of the ability to prove it. In fact, this suspension of disbelief is the very root of what we adults call faith. After all, an adult's belief in God is primarily based on faith. And conversely, the decision to not believe in a higher being is based on a lack of evidence of such a being—you choose not to have faith without evidence. Your child's questions about what God makes are the first signs that he is grappling with this dilemma.

The Best Way to Respond

Once again, and remaining consistent within this category, the best way to respond to this question is to begin by asking your child what he believes. In fact, by responding to this particular question often enough in this way, you will force your child to begin formulating his own thoughts on the subject of what God makes, rather than automatically asking you for the answer, and he will likely stop asking you the question as often. Helping your child to develop independent thinking is healthy under any circumstance, and it is particularly useful when he is asking you a repetitive question to which there is not necessarily a clear-cut answer.

If he insists on you giving him an answer (either by continually asking, or because you see that his level of anxiety is increased rather than decreased by not getting a concrete response from you), your response should, of course, take into account your beliefs about God—because these are what you would like your child to learn. But at the same time, your response should not be so rigid or specific that your child is dissuaded from personal thoughts or ideas.

A good example of a response (if you believe in God) may be something similar to the following: "God helps people to become creative and smart. A person worked hard to make that car, but God helped him by giving him the smart brain to figure out how to do it." This is open-ended enough to allow your child to believe in God but also to understand that one still needs to take responsibility for his behavior in order to be successful in life. In the case of a naturally occurring event, you may want explain that "God created that beautiful mountain, but people need to make sure that they take care of nature so that it stays beautiful."

An alternate response (if you don't believe in God as a creator) might be, "People are very smart, and they are good at thinking of things for themselves. It was a smart, hard-working person who created and built that car." This response doesn't outright negate God as a creator (which you can choose to add if you feel strongly about it), but it demonstrates to your child that people's actions (or those of nature) are responsible for creation.

#27: IS GOD A BOY OR A GIRL?

"When Sierra (age 5) asked me whether God was a girl or a boy, I couldn't believe it!" remarked Sierra's dad, Ben.

"I never imagined she would have such deep thoughts, but it was really exciting to see her brain beginning to work like that."

I love this question! It demonstrates that your child is really beginning to think in a complex and philosophical way about life. You can almost see the wheels turning. The problem shared by many parents is that they are not always sure how to respond to this question. Do *you* know whether God is a boy or a girl, a man or a woman? Does anyone know for sure?

Uncovering the Meaning

Believe it or not, this question represents a much more complex developmental issue than you may recognize on the surface. It is about God, but it is also about much more. So get ready, because I'm about to offer you another psychological insight into your child's emotional growth that you'll find fascinating.

To begin this discussion, you will find it useful to read Chapter Six, Question #32, "Can I marry you when I'm grown up?" Don't forget to come right back here when you are done.

As you see, around four or five years old, children begin to develop a strong identity with their own genders. We see this in the way they play, in the way they choose to dress, and in that they begin to notice the difference between boys' and girls' bodies (see Chapter Eight, Question #42, "Why does he have a penis and I don't?")

It therefore makes sense that your child's interest in gender extends to God. As she is beginning to learn to understand and categorize everyone (including pets, stuffed animals, and even other toys) into correct genders, she wants to know how God fits into this newly discovered pattern as well. However, since no one has ever seen God, some parents aren't sure how to respond.

In addition, although much religious writing refers to God as "He," many people are reluctant to ascribe a human gender to God, believing that "He" was the default language used in biblical writing, and that in reality God is actually different from or more than either man or woman, so that neither one of these terms is truly accurate.

That being said, some people read the Bible literally and do believe strongly that God is male. Of course, given that we have no proof either way, there is clearly no right or wrong answer to this question. Maintaining this nonjudgmental attitude is the most important element to convey to your child when you respond to this question, regardless of what you believe.

The Best Way to Respond

From a developmental perspective, it is best to offer your child a response that indicates that God is neither a boy nor a girl, but rather, since God is not a human being, we cannot talk about God like we talk about people. Alternatively, you might say that we don't know whether God is a girl or a boy and ask, "What do you think?" Then accept your child's response as satisfactory for now. This approach is best for either a girl or a boy going through the stage of gender self-identification. It will help your child's confidence and sense of self, knowing that she can identify God with herself.

If you feel religiously compelled to identify God as male, it is important to explain to your child that God is a boy because he is like a father that we can't see, one who takes care of all of us. Both young boys and girls need to understand that God being male does not mean that he favors boys in any way. You can explain this by telling a version of the following to your child: "Daddies can have sons and daughters (use your own or another family as an example). They love their girls and boys just the same. That's what God does too."

#28: WHY DO I HAVE TO GO TO RELIGIOUS SCHOOL?

"I get this question from Timothy (age 6) and Bonnie (age 8) every week, several times a week," said their mother, Diana. "I'm not really sure how to answer them...I found religious school boring when I was a kid. I hated having to come home from regular school and then go to religious school classes and then also go again to Sunday school, so I don't blame them for disliking it. I admit that it's hard for me to give them a convincing reason why they need to go."

Ah, yes, the complaints about religious school do begin young! But if you don't confront and deal with them right now, they'll simply get worse as your child gets older. What is it about religious school that children dislike so much, and is there anything you can do about it?

Uncovering the Meaning

Believe it or not, there are several possible reasons your child could dislike religious school at such a young age:

- He is overburdened with too many activities and would rather not go to religious school and give up another, more fun activity.
- You subtly convey that religious school is not fun or that it is boring (based on your own negative experience as a child). Your child notices your lack of conviction and embraces it as his own.
- The religious school your child attends really *isn't* fun or it *is* boring. Sometimes children behave badly at religious school, and the teachers don't have the training or desire to control them. This makes the experience unpleasant for all the children, even for those who want to enjoy it and learn.
- You don't connect religious school with religion. If you never attend religious services, your child will not find meaning in the classes he is taking. The more connected your family is to your house

of worship, the more comfortable your child will be attending classes and the more valuable he will find them. This is true now and becomes even more so as your child gets older. Your child will challenge you even more when he is a preteen or a teenager if you are rarely or never involved in your house of worship, but yet expect your child to be. He will view you as a hypocrite; he won't be wrong.

- If your child has a learning issue that is addressed in regular school, accommodations for it also need to be made in religious school, or your child will feel overwhelmed, unhappy, or confused.
- Your child is simply testing your limits to see how far he can push you.

At this young age, if your child complains consistently about religious school, it is important to understand why he is doing so and to address the problem. If you don't, it will only get worse, and your child will grow to resent religious school even more—except of course for the last point, which requires you to set a firm limit and stick to it.

The Best Way to Respond

When addressing this issue with your child, you need to be clear about your priorities. For example, if religious school (and attending services) is important to you, but your child is overburdened, then you need to cut down on other activities. This is an important message to give your child. By doing so you are telling him that nurturing his soul is at least as important as fueling his brain and body. In fact, you can actually tell him this with words. By allowing him to sometimes miss religious school for sports or other activities, you give a clear message that this is not a priority for you. Don't expect him to then make it a priority for himself. What's more, remember B. F. Skinner's operant conditioning theory from Chapter Three, Question #15: If you give in sometimes, your child will increase his attempts to try and get you to give in all the time.

Finding the right house of worship for your family that also meets the needs of your young child will send your child the message that it is important to you that he have a satisfying experience. What's more, you may find that the right place will change your attitude toward religious school. You may have had a negative experience as a child, but if you find the right environment—with lots of other young families who are enthusiastic and a school that keeps kids interested—you might change your mind and want to spend more time there too.

If your child has a learning issue, you should make sure you meet with the teachers at the religious school to explain to them how they can best meet your child's needs. You may need to be more involved than you would be in regular school in order to provide them with support and help.

If your child is simply pushing your buttons or testing limits by refusing to go, you need to stand firm. Like any other situation, if this is important to you, then your child needs to understand that you are not going to give in. If his behavior is unacceptable, appropriate consequences should be meted out.

6

Step-by-Step Separation

Beginning with your child's first steps, you saw signs of the emerging conflict between wanting to separate from you and being fearful to do so. She took a couple of steps away and then quickly jumped back into your arms.

As with all other areas of development, each child becomes comfortable with separation at a different rate. One child may be ready to sleep at her grandparent's home—or even a friend's—by the time she is four, while another may not be ready for this until a few years later. It is an unpredictable process, and parents often expect it to be over by the early elementary years. However, very often it isn't.

You may be surprised to discover that for a great many children, the struggle to feel comfortable leaving Mom or Dad's side is no easy task, even into the elementary years. Fueled by newfound fears (see Chapter Four), as well as rapidly changing school and social lives, many preschool- and early-elementary-age children go through a stage when they become less willing to separate from their parents than they had been just a short while before. For this reason, you will likely find that many of the questions in this chapter are familiar.

#29: CAN I SLEEP IN YOUR BED? (OR: CAN YOU STAY WITH ME UNTIL I FALL ASLEEP? CAN YOU SLEEP WITH ME? CAN I SLEEP ON YOUR FLOOR?)

"I'm exhausted!" declared Daisy. "I thought that the baby years would be the most difficult, but Tori is five and she still asks to sleep in my bed practically every night. If I say no, she starts to cry. She may get so hysterical that it's hard to calm her down enough for her to go to sleep at all. It's not worth it, so I let her sleep with us, but she moves around and kicks, so I don't get much sleep. Sometimes I lie in her bed with her until she falls asleep instead, which I know isn't any better. And then she may wake up in the middle of the night and come into our bed anyway. I don't know what to do!"

Going to sleep is one of the most common transition times during which a young child will express her difficulties with separation. However, it also represents a crucial parenting opportunity—a time for you to show your child that she can learn how to help herself when she feels worried and anxious about a natural separation like sleep. Once you understand this particular question, you will feel more confident in your ability to manage it in a manner that will help your child grow in an emotionally healthy way.

Uncovering the Meaning

Like Tori, many children did not learn as infants how to soothe themselves to fall asleep or stay asleep. Even as they entered their later babyhood and toddler years, they didn't figure out how to do this. If yours is such a child, the reason she did not learn this skill (and it *is* a skill) might be because you—perhaps unwittingly—didn't teach it to her by allowing her to soothe herself to sleep by crying a bit. Or perhaps you did, but she's somehow unlearned it along the way due to nightmares, teething, or another childhood interruption. So now, in the preschool and early elementary years, your child still doesn't know how to help herself fall asleep at night without your help.

Although there are different schools of thought on this issue, I strongly urge you to recognize that learning how to sleep through the night, in one's own space, without needing another person to soothe you to sleep, is a *critical* life skill. When you allow your child to sleep with you, or when you fall asleep with her, you deprive her of the opportunity to learn how to develop her own ability to cope with the momentary frustration of being alone or not being able to fall asleep, and needing to learn how to soothe herself. *Learning frustration tolerance and self-soothing are at the core of becoming a tolerant, patient, accepting child and adult.*

When your child has a temper tantrum because you said no to something, it is largely because she doesn't have the ability to employ self-soothing skills when she's frustrated by not getting what she wants. When a teen lashes out rudely and impulsively at a peer or an adult in a socially inappropriate manner, it's because she has never learned self-soothing skills. And when a teen or an adult yells, becomes verbally abusive, or even escalates to physical aggression, it's because no one taught that individual how to manage her feelings appropriately and deal with a frustrating situation calmly.

Of course not learning to sleep through the night by oneself is not the sole reason for all these behaviors. But learning to soothe oneself to sleep is a very important stepping stone along the path of self-soothing skills necessary for coping with all frustrating situations.

Often, a child learns to soothe herself to sleep for the first time in infancy, although it may not happen until she is a toddler. If your child hasn't learned yet, it isn't too late to teach her, and, as I've explained, it is very, very important.

By asking if she can sleep with you, your child is letting you know that she doesn't have confidence in her own ability to meet her own needs, and that she is relying on you to meet them for her. But by giving in to her, you give her the message that you don't have much confidence in her either. Is this what you want your child to feel? I didn't think so. You need to break the cycle. I'll show you how next.

The Best Way to Respond

To begin, this is a marathon, not a sprint. If you have been helping your child to fall asleep or fall back asleep in the middle of the night for years, then teaching her to sleep alone may be a bit challenging, because she won't like it at first.

The next time she asks you this question, respond by saying, "We're making a new rule in our family—everybody sleeps in their own beds. I'm going to help you do it." If you already have a similar rule, but you haven't been enforcing it, then say, "From now on, we're going to stick to the rule that everyone sleeps in their own beds, and I'm going to help you do it."

After you have responded to the question by explaining the rule, the trick will be to be consistent. This is the most important and the most challenging part. If your child is very upset by the idea of falling asleep completely alone, it is fine to begin by sitting in a chair next to your child's bed for a few nights. Over a period of a week or two, you should move your chair closer and closer to the door a few inches each night, until eventually, at the end of a week or two, it is out the door. At this point, your child does not need you anymore. If this takes longer than a week or two, it is fine, but stick with it, no matter what.

If your child comes to your room during the night to try and sleep in your bed, you *must* take your child back to her bed—no matter how tired you are! Even if your child has a bad dream that has awakened her during the night, comfort her and take her back to her own bed. The message must be clear: "It is just a dream; it can't hurt you." If you allow your child to stay in your bed at night, it will become a habit—bad dreams or not! The only way she will get the message that she needs to sleep in her own bed is if you enforce it.

Many parents wonder about the difference between nightmares and night terrors. Night terrors most often arise during early childhood (although they can occur at any time during life). They differ from nightmares in that they take place during a different stage of sleep (non-REM stage) than nightmares (REM stage), and they are not experienced as dreams at all. Rather, the person awakens with the feeling of fear or panic, rather than any memory of a dream. They can also be scary for a parent, because a child often screams, thrashes around, sweats, experiences rapid heart rate, and awakens suddenly. A child often goes through a short phase when he has several night terrors and then has no more. Their occurrence can be genetic—passed from parent to child. Stress and being overtired can also trigger night terrors.

A technique that really works to help a child stay in her bed during the night is to give the child a clock next to her bed. Tell her that if she wakes up during the night (unless she feels sick or has a nightmare that requires comforting), she needs to stay in her bed until she counts ten (or twenty) minutes on the clock—teach her how to do this. In most cases, she will fall back asleep long before then because counting ten minutes on a clock is quite taxing for a young child. This will not only break her of the habit of coming in to you, it will also reprogram her sleep cycle, so that she doesn't come to full wakefulness during the night and get out of bed.

As you are teaching your child to sleep in her own space, it is important to be aware of your own feelings about separating from your child during sleep. In many cases, the reason you have been allowing your child to sleep in your bed, or you have been falling asleep with your child, is in part because it is not just your child who has trouble separating. It is likely that you too are ambivalent about giving up the very strong connection of infancy—the one that means that your child is completely dependent on you. It is in your child's best interest for him to sleep in his own space, to learn to soothe himself to sleep and back to sleep if he wakes up in the night. If you feel ambivalent about your child's growing independence, it is important not to allow this to interfere with your child's emotional growth by preventing you from teaching him this very important skill.

#30: WILL YOU NOT GO OUT TONIGHT? (OR: DO YOU HAVE TO GO OUT? WILL YOU STAY HOME THIS TIME?)

Nancy, whose middle child, Alex, is six, explains the typical Friday night scenario in her home with Alex: "It might include gentle asking beginning early in the day, which rises to a hysterical crescendo of begging as the night approaches and I begin to dress for a night on the town (four hours for dinner and a movie)."

Fear of separation very often rears its head when parents plan a few hours out alone on a Friday or Saturday night—even for kids who are solidly secure at all other times.

Uncovering the Meaning

The fast-paced changes that accompany becoming a newly independent, "grown up kid"—the oldest in the nursery school, on the verge of change, and then the move and adjustment to a big kid school—can trigger feelings of insecurity for a child who might believe he isn't quite ready to feel grown up just yet. These feelings will most likely be expressed when you plan to go out at night because your child is tired and because the regular routine of you putting him to sleep is being changed (although they can occur anytime). They can continue through the early elementary years and even beyond, if you don't respond to them effectively.

It is also important to note that a vulnerable child's reaction can also be improved or exacerbated by the type of childcare provider you employ. A fun, nurturing, engaged sitter will be much more likely to diffuse a child's anxious feelings than one who is quiet, unenthusiastic, or businesslike. In addition, an English language (or another language primary to your child) baby-sitter can also make a difference, because if your child cannot communicate effectively with the childcare provider, the feeling of being all alone and not well understood will greatly increase the separation anxiety.

In many cases, a child experiences anticipatory anxiety as soon as he finds out about your plans. This frequently peaks in hysterical crying at the moment of separation, but then once you have left, a surreptitious call to the sitter reveals that your child was completely fine as soon as the door closed behind you. This is valuable information! It tells you that your child's begging and pleading definitely *should not* result in you changing your plans. In fact, you should go out on a regular basis to help your child become accustomed to these moments of separation, knowing that another adult can take good care of him in your absence.

The Best Way to Respond

When speaking to your child, always be clear that his asking, nagging, whining, and tantrums will not change your plans. Respond to this question by saying something similar to the following: "I know you would like me to stay home, but you have plenty of time to play with your friends at the playground, at recess, at their houses, and at parties. This is my time for fun. You will be very well taken care of and when I come home I will come in to your room and kiss you while you sleep."

If necessary you can add, "It doesn't matter how many times you ask or yell, it is not going to change my mind, but it may make me angry if you're disrespectful or out of control. If you can do a good job saying good-bye to me tonight, the baby-sitter can give you a treat. If you have a fit, then she can't." The treat should be something small, and it should be something that the baby-sitter offers while you are out, such as a DVD to watch, or a fun art project to do together. You should decide the treat and have it ready prior to the evening, based on what motivates your child. Tell your child about it in advance so he is clear about the incentive to control his behavior.

Of course, if you have any hint—a gut feeling even (remember, I believe in these!)—that your child is responding negatively to something in the child-care provider, or that the child-care provider has treated your child in a way with which you don't feel absolutely comfortable, you should not force your child to stay with this person, no matter how much you want to go out.

#31: DO YOU HAVE TO GO TO WORK?

Diana explained her plight: "My kids hate that I work! Rosie (age 18 months), the baby, is fine so far, but Ralphie (age 4) and Rebecca (age 6) complain several times a week. They make me feel guilty, saying that they hardly ever see me, that I'm never there after school and 'How come all the other moms are around?' It's awful! I used to enjoy working, but not anymore."

This, in a nutshell, is the plight of many mothers who work outside the home. You are torn between needing to work, either for financial reasons or for reasons of self-satisfaction, and feeling that by doing so you are somehow not meeting the emotional needs of your child. When your child ask you this question—especially when she does so frequently—it *really* tugs at your heartstrings. But what does the question actually mean and how should you answer it so that both your child and you feel satisfied?

Uncovering the Meaning

Let's begin by clarifying two issues:

1. Work can be paid or volunteer—many women do extraordinary work for their communities, schools, or other organizations for which they are not paid. If you are doing meaningful work outside your home, either to financially support your family or

to contribute to the greater good of your world, it is worthwhile work for the purpose of this discussion.

2. If you so choose, you are entitled to work for the sole purpose of satisfying your desire to have an identity other than that of a mother. You should exercise this entitlement with no feelings of guilt or pressure to stay home. On the other hand, you are also entitled (if finances allow) to *not* work and you should exercise this entitlement to be a stay-at-home mother with no feelings of guilt or pressure to work. Of course, working part-time—the compromise—is an option that satisfies many mothers. You should not expend energy judging the choices that other mothers make. After working with thousands of mothers, I tell you with confidence that being a good mother has *nothing* to do with whether or not you work. I know many stay-at-home moms doing an abysmal job raising their children and just as many superb full-time working moms.

Now to the question. In some cases, a child is unhappy that you work because the alternative childcare arrangement isn't satisfying for her. As we discussed in the prior question, the type of child care you have can either enhance or decrease your child's feelings of missing you while you are at work. Many parents engage daily child care that is convenient, inexpensive, easy, and, of course, trustworthy. But sometimes this combination doesn't take into account that childcare is not a situation that your child enjoys.

For example, perhaps Diana has a slightly older grandparent caring for her three kids. The basics may be covered, but Ralphie and Rebecca may not have someone to help with homework, negotiate arguments, or really run after the baby. In addition, maybe Grandma doesn't let them play outside because she can't watch all of them. This may be stressful for the kids. No wonder they want Mom at home.

As another example, perhaps the sitter is a non-English-speaking housekeeper who makes dinner, cleans, and takes care of the baby, but doesn't really interact with the older children other than to give them meals and make sure they take baths. This is not much fun for them either, and it's also a bit chaotic because they run circles around her when it comes to discipline.

In other situations a child is unhappy because she perceives herself to be the only child whose mom works. Of course, this is never the case, but a very young child will have a difficult time seeing beyond her own small world.

Last, your child may feel that your work takes up all your time, even when you are home. This will surely cause her to feel that she wants to cling to you, rather than letting you go to work. It is important to ask yourself if this is the case. Answer these questions honestly: While at home, do you spend a lot of time on the phone (for either work or pleasure)? Are you on the computer a great deal? Do you find that you are not fully focused on your child (or children)? A child's resentment about a parent working often stems from feeling that the parent never leaves work at work. *Even nonworking parents should answer these questions!*

It is your job to make sure that your child feels your time with her is valuable to you. The way you respond to the question will show her that even though you work she is still your first priority.

The Best Way to Respond

As you can tell from the prior section, before responding to this question, it is vital that you assess your childcare situation and if necessary make changes that are in the best interest of your child—even if they are difficult changes to make. Perhaps your child would be better in an after-school program, or with a younger, more energetic baby-sitter. Maybe you need to arrange to pay another mom in the neighborhood to watch your children. It is possible that you need to be really innovative and come up with some combination of arrangements to satisfy your budget and your child's emotional needs.

Once you are truly satisfied that your child is in the best possible childcare situation that you can work out, then it is possible to respond to the question with confidence. Keep in mind that it is healthy for children, both girls and boys, to see their moms and dads work (whether it is paid or volunteer work). You role-model for your child that we need to work hard to get the things that we want financially, that we give back to the world, and that it feels good to use our brains and our bodies to create and produce. *Every child needs to learn these lessons.* In preschool and the early elementary years, you are your child's best example.

So, when your child asks this question, answer with conviction and a smile on your face, offering a variation of the following: "Yes, I do have to go to work. I want to go to work; it's important to me and people are counting on me there. My work means a lot to me and I really like it. Work makes my brain strong, just like school makes your brain strong. It also keeps my body strong—just like school does for you. But when I come home later, you will tell me all about school, and I will tell you all about work, and we will play a game together and have dinner."

When you are home with your child, in the mornings, evenings, and on weekends, here are five tips so your child feels that your time together is valuable. These will go a long way toward reducing your child's desire that you not work:

- Take your phone/PDA off your body while you are with your child.
- Go on the computer only after your child is asleep at night.
- Take your child with you to run errands (super-market, dry cleaner, drugstore, etc.).

- If you have more than one child, once a week create one-on-one time with each child—even for an hour.

- Limit social phone calls to times that your child is sleeping or otherwise engaged. Make weekend days family time and save grown-up socializing for the night. In fact, it is a good idea to allow the answering machine or voicemail to pick up when the phone rings at night until after your child or children are tucked into bed.

#32: CAN I MARRY YOU WHEN I'M GROWN UP?

Serena explains the frequent conversation she has with her son William: "Willy (age 4) is so cute! He always asks me if we can get married. Sometimes I say, 'But you're too little,' and he'll respond, 'But when I'm big, then you can marry *me*!' What should I say to that?"

Many young children, although by no means all, go through a phase during which they become very interested in spending time with the opposite-sex parents and even show signs of feeling threatened by their same-sex parents. This question reflects that phase and is a normal and very interesting part of child development.

Uncovering the Meaning

This question has its fascinating roots embedded in the psychological world. Beginning around three years old and ending around five or six, children go through a period made famous by Sigmund Freud, often known as the Oedipal stage. Based on the conventions of the era in which he studied and wrote, Freud focused only on boys in his description of the Oedipal stage. Many of Freud's theories have since been debunked (including certain aspects of the Oedipal phase itself), but since this particular one is so frequently seen in young children—both boys and girls—it is worth understanding. A boy going through this period typically becomes enamored with his mother and wants to "steal her" from his father. In psychological terms, a young boy will identify with the male characteristics of his father—begin acting "male"—in order to garner his mother's attention. Eventually this phase is resolved when the young boy realizes that he won't be able to take his mom away from his dad, but instead he allies himself with his father, and thus his male identity is formed.

A similar phase attributed to young girls was described later by psychoanalyst Carl Jung (based on Freud's work), and is known as the Electra complex. During this stage a little girl is attracted to her father and resents her mother. It resolves with her identifying with the female characteristics of her mother. However, many people refer to the phase in both boys and girls as Oedipal—which is what I will do here.

While going through this stage, a child engages in behaviors that make his feelings clear to his parents. This question is a common indication that he is going through this phase. There are other signs that reflect your child's passing through the Oedipal phase, including:

- He asks to sleep in your bed with you *in place of Dad* ("Can I sleep with you, and Daddy can sleep in my bed?").
- He exhibits aggressive behavior toward Dad—punching, kicking, wanting to "beat him up" (girls are more likely to demonstrate verbally "mean" behavior toward Mom).
- He pushes between you and his dad when he sees you hugging, holding hands, sitting together, or otherwise showing affection toward each other.

The way you respond to this question, as well as to the other Oedipal behaviors that arise, is important because your management of this issue can either help or delay your child's ability to move through the Oedipal stage in a healthy manner. Wondering why? Read on.

The Best Way to Respond

Now that I've explained the Oedipal stage, it will make sense when I now tell you that in order for your child to reach the end of the Oedipal phase in a complete and healthy way, he first needs to learn that he can't have the power to "steal" his mom from his dad (or, for a girl, her dad from her mom). Therefore the way you respond to this question needs to be clear, with a variation of the following: "I love you very much because you are my little boy, but I am married to Daddy. I love being married to Daddy—he is my husband and I will always be married to Daddy. One day, when you are very big, you will find someone to marry whom you love. And I will be very excited to meet her!"

In addition to responding to this question clearly, it is also important that your child understands that he can't get between Mom and Dad at other times. For example, it is never advisable for one parent to leave the bed in order for a child to sleep there. Even in cases of illness, where you feel that you need to have your child sleeping near you, I strongly suggest that you set up an extra bed for your child (or you sleep in your child's room on a separate mattress). Children—even those past the typical Oedipal phase—will very easily begin to feel that they have the power to kick their parents out of bed and replace them. No child should have this much power. If your child is physically or verbally aggressive, it is appropriate to stop the behavior immediately and establish consequences.

Likewise, you should not allow your child to push between you regularly if he is trying to break apart your affectionate moments. Handle this in two ways: First, verbally, by one of you saying, "Mommy and I like to hug and kiss so please don't stop us"; second, with body language—for example if your child jumps between you on the couch, gently move him to one side. Your message needs to be sensitive, but consistent and clear: your adult relationship is safe and he cannot break it up. Ultimately, this is what he wants to know. It would be very unsettling for him, at such a young age, to feel that he had such power to break up his parents' relationship.

#33: CAN I LIVE WITH YOU FOREVER?

"Janey (age 6) sometimes climbs into bed with us on a Saturday morning and says, 'I want to live with you forever! Can I? I don't ever want anything to change.'" Janey's mom, Brigitte, is conflicted about how to respond to her. " I'm never sure what to say. I'm afraid that if I say, 'Sure, you can stay here forever,' she'll take me up on it! But if I say, 'When you're a big girl, you'll go to college,' she'll get upset and nervous."

It is hard to imagine that your adorable little child will one day grow up and want to live on her own. But don't blink, because before you know it, she'll be a teenager and talking about college or her own apartment—or at the very least, she'll be keeping her door closed so often that you'll think she moved out. But for now, she loves her home.

Uncovering the Meaning

A young child doesn't have the cognitive capacity to think about the far future—probably not much past next week, depending on her age. She also can't imagine what she will be like when she is in her late teens. Even an older child doesn't yet have the capacity to picture how she will change as she matures. Some teens still can't imagine that they might be completely different in a few years than they are right now. And the parents of teens have a hard time imagining this too, which is why outlandish clothes, black nail polish, and spiked hair drive them crazy!

It is therefore almost impossible for a preschool- or early-elementary-age child to picture herself living anywhere but with you. However, since she probably observes older children—perhaps a college-age cousin, or an older neighbor—moving away from home, she may become concerned that you will expect her to do the same. Therefore, when she asks you this question it is meant to elicit a comforting response from you, one that will allay any worry that you will make her move out. But don't forget, she is basing her concern on who she is right now because that's all she's capable of imagining. She can't conceive that someday she will be able to take care of all her needs, manage money, make independent choices, and do her own laundry...Okay, maybe I've gone a bit too far, but you know what I mean! Nevertheless, since she doesn't yet have the cognitive capacity to understand that she will someday possess these skills, you won't be able to convince her that she will eventually be able to manage these things—and that in all likelihood will be thrilled to move out (probably long before you're ready for her to do so).

The Best Way to Respond

Although it is unlikely that your child will remember your exact response forever, it is certainly possible (I have known young children who have remembered all sorts of things their parents have told them), so you do want to be careful how you phrase this response. Therefore, saying, "Yes, you can absolutely live with me forever!" may be comforting, but it will paint you into an uncomfortable corner if you do at some point want your young adult child to move out and become independent and self-supporting.

On the other hand, now that you understand that your child cannot imagine living anywhere but with you, it would not be prudent to suggest to her that "One day, when you're big, you will want to move out, so don't worry about it now," or "All kids move out when they grow up." A response like one of these might create real anxiety for your child.

The best response to a child this age to this question— or a similar one—is a variation of the following: "You're my child and I love you so much, which means that you will always have a home wherever I am! And if you ever decide to explore anywhere else even for a short time— like having a sleepover at someone's house or going to camp for a few days—you will always come back to your home here with me."

The two elements that are important in this response are first, that your child always has a home with you (which will alleviate any concern), and second, that you are suggesting that she should begin to explore the idea of separating from you in an age-appropriate way and that this doesn't conflict with feeling safe at home. If your child tries to get a concrete answer from you, it is absolutely fine to tell her that this is not a conversation you need to have until she is older.

7

Does Money Grow on Trees?

Doesn't it sometimes seem that your child was born to spend your money? The "Will you buy me's?" and "Can you get me's?" are endless! Even a child as young as three or four asks mom or dad to get out the cash and spend it on him.

It can be exhausting to feel like you are always deciding when to say yes, and when to say no and then to possibly deal with a sulking child when you don't say yes. Most importantly it is not fun to always have empty pockets because your child or children have convinced you—once again—to spend your last few dollars on junk at the supermarket checkout.

Guess what? Teaching your child to value *your* money is important. In addition, the questions he asks about money reflect his beginning interest in understanding the way money impacts his life. By taking the time to answer his questions the right way now, when he is very young, you will help him begin to appreciate the value of money and the way it impacts his life and the lives of others. With any luck, you will help him enter the next stage of development (the later elementary years) with a greater appreciation for and understanding of money. If you are *really* fortunate—and are consistent in teaching these early lessons—your child will spend the rest of his childhood and adolescence appreciating and valuing the money and material possessions you give him, rather than expecting them as his due.

#34: CAN YOU BUY ME _____ [FILL IN THE BLANK]?

Tonya and Isaac, the parents of Jada (age 4), Nikki (age 7), and Jayson (age 9), dread taking their children into a store of any kind. "It doesn't matter whether it's the supermarket, drugstore, or even a hardware store, they find something they must have," explained Isaac, exasperated.

"And if you say no to them they whine, pout, or beg," continued Tonya. "I refuse to take them to a toy store. That's the worst of all!"

Does this sound familiar to you? Many parents feel exactly like Isaac and Tonya. This was one of the most frequently submitted questions, not only for this age group, but for all of them. Children plague their parents with requests morning, noon, and night, and some parents don't know what to do about it.

It takes hard work and consistency to help your child move beyond the "buy me, buy me" phase. But you can do it. And when you start this young—*and stick with it*—you're much more likely to be successful.

Uncovering the Meaning

A child in this age range, especially at the younger end of it, is too young to grasp the real value of money. Therefore, when she asks you to buy her something— whether it is a pack of gum, a small toy, or a pony—she does not recognize the different monetary values of each of these items. A child at the top range of this age group (a seven- or eight-year-old) is beginning to grasp the value of money in a limited sense, so she may understand that a pack of gum is worth less than a pony, but she still won't understand how much less, or what this difference truly means in your family.

When a young child asks you to buy her something, the question actually has very little to do with her appreciation for the value of money, and much more to do with her desire or impulse to own the item. She is old enough to recognize that a transaction must take place (the exchange of money) before she can walk out of the store with the item she desires. But she can't quite comprehend why this exchange should upset you. A concept that you take for granted (money is valuable, and we don't just spend it on frivolous items) makes no sense to her when she really wants the candy or toy (so why can't you just take out the paper or coins and give them to the person behind the counter so she can have the item she wants?).

A young child will also ask you to buy her something she has seen on TV or at a friend's house. Here, too, she is not thinking about the cost, only about the item she wants.

The Best Way to Respond

In truth, during the younger ages of this stage (three to five years old), your goal is to teach your child to manage her frustration when you say no. It is not really about teaching her to understand the value of money. If *you* become outwardly frustrated or angry with your child for asking you to buy her something (even if it happens often), rather than using this as a learning opportunity, it will interfere with your ability to teach her to manage her frustration. A negative response to her behavior will role-model poor frustration tolerance as an acceptable response when one is unhappy (which may be part of the reason your child behaves this way too). Remember, she doesn't understand the concept of spending money, and being angry with her for not valuing it is not going to make her understand it any faster.

As your child moves through the older end of this stage (six to eight years old) you can begin to introduce the concept of spending money and connect it to the way you respond to her requests to you to buy, buy, buy. Once again, patience and consistency will afford you the best opportunity to teach your child about money and saving.

The following are seven tips to help you manage this question most effectively:

1. Before walking into a store with your child, be clear that you are not going to be buying her anything—and then stick to the plan. You can't blame your child for begging you to buy, buy, buy, if it sometimes pays off (see Chapter One, "Nag, Nag, Nag"). Respond to this question with a firm no each and every time, unless you and your child have discussed the purchase before entering the store and it is not an impulse buy.

2. Do not reward good behavior with toys, candy, or other "gifts," especially while shopping. Your child will become used to getting gifts for good behavior—this is a bad habit. Good behavior is its own reward, and poor behavior should have a negative consequence! Remind your child of this before entering every store.

3. There is no rule that requires you to purchase a "small gift" for your child when you are at the toy store purchasing a gift for someone else. This is an opportunity for your child to learn about giving, not receiving. Remind your child of this before you walk into the store.

4. When your child asks for an item seen on TV or owned by someone else, do not say, "We'll see" or "Maybe" and then ignore the issue, especially if you actually mean no. Discuss the subject directly with your child, giving her a finite response—either yes or no, depending on whether you believe it to be a valuable purchase, not based on your child harassing you. If you are not ready to decide immediately, tell your child that you will think about it and let her know when you have decided, and that she should not ask again.

5. When you child is old enough to begin understanding the concept of money, your "no" responses to this question should start to include phrases similar to one of the following:
   - "That is too much money."
   - "Today we have enough money for food we need but not for candy that we don't need."
   - "I spent money on gum for you yesterday. That is enough money for gum in one week. Next week we can buy gum again."
   - "There won't be money in my wallet to spend on toys until Christmas—that's in two months. We can mark it on the calendar, so you won't need to keep asking before that."

6. Most children in this age range are still too young to understand and value an allowance. In Chapter Seven of *The Top 50 Questions Kids Ask (3rd*

through 5th Grade), we discuss allowances extensively. So if your child is at the top end of the age range of this book (or if you have an older child), pick up a copy of the next one.

7. Give your child pretend money and a register to play "store." Playing will help her learn to understand the give and take of money for goods (although it's unlikely that she will understand the actual value of money—other than coins being worth less than paper money).

#35: I HAVE $2 IN MY BANK. CAN I BUY A TOY?

This question, usually asked by a six- or seven-year-old, helps you realize the true limitations of a young child's understanding of the value of money. "Cooper (age 7½) will bring me all the money he has been saving, expecting to be able to buy something big—a video game or a fabulous toy he saw on TV that I wouldn't buy him," explains Cooper's mom, Carrie. "Then he gets frustrated when I tell him it's not nearly enough for what he wants to purchase. He gets mad at me, as if it's my fault that he doesn't have enough money."

How should Carrie—or any parent—help her child avoid this type of frustration? It's a slow learning process.

Uncovering the Meaning

As with the question above, your child does not yet grasp the value of money. He also can't properly place a value on how much things cost. He simply doesn't have the cognitive ability yet to be able to think in these complex terms. In fact, young children believe that the more "pieces" of money they have, the richer they are—regardless of whether they have a pile of pennies or quarters, a stack of singles or tens. In fact, even some older children still struggle a little with this concept. I know ten- and eleven-year-olds who know that a ten-dollar bill is exactly the same as ten singles, but they always ask their parents for ten singles. They say it just makes them "feel" wealthier!

In case you were wondering, there is a cool psychological concept that explains why children do this, so let me share it with you.

Jean Piaget studied children and discovered a theory of cognitive development that is still highly influential today. One aspect of his theory is called conservation. Conservation is the ability to know that an object or an amount is still the same even if it changes its form. A common illustration of conservation is when you pour liquid from a short, squat glass into a tall, skinny one. A child who has not yet developed the cognitive ability to understand conservation will think that there is more liquid in the second glass, even if you poured it right in front of him. A child who understands conservation will know that it is the same amount of liquid, even though it looks like more. Other examples of conservation are rolling a piece of clay to look bigger and flatter and laying one row of blocks out so it looks longer than another row of exactly the same number of blocks.

Now, let's think about money. A young child (not yet able cognitively to understand conservation) will have a difficult time seeing that one quarter is more money than ten pennies, or that one dollar is the same as four quarters, or that four one-dollar bills is less than one five-dollar bill. It makes sense now that you understand it cognitively, right? I told you it was cool! Therefore, the money your child is studiously collecting in his wallet or piggy bank will seem like a whole lot more to him than it really is. Helping him avoid disappointment requires planning.

The Best Way to Respond

If you are aware that your child is trying to save for something unrealistically expensive, it is a good idea to discuss this with him right away, rather than waiting for him to come to you, having already created high expectations. Let him down gently, using terms that he can understand. For example, you might say: "You would need about forty dollar bills—a pile this high—in order to buy that game. You don't have enough money for that. But you do have enough money right here, these two dollars, to buy yourself that red dinosaur pen you liked in the drugstore the other day. Or you could keep saving it for something really special."

I encourage you not to feel sorry for your child when he realizes that he can't afford something he wants. In addition, it is definitely not in your child's best interest to buy him the item he wants, even though he can't afford it—*not* now and *not* when he is older! Disappointment is part of life, and learning how to cope with it is a critical part of maturing into an emotionally healthy older child, teenager, and adult. *If you always short-circuit your child's opportunity to work through this feeling (by buying him whatever he wants), you practically guarantee that you are raising a child that you—and everyone else—will eventually dislike.*

#36: ARE WE RICH?

"Kayla (age 6) seems to be so concerned with whether or not we are rich," Kayla's dad, Eric, told me. "She asks me the question all the time, often for no reason. What do kids talk about in school these days?"

There's no doubt about it, we live in a materialistic culture, and kids—even little kids as young as five or six—think about, discuss, and compare their families' wealth. It is unpleasant to think about, but it's true. What does it all mean, and what can you do about it?

Uncovering the Meaning

You have heard the phrase before: Children are like sponges—they soak up information and knowledge. Your child hears talk about "being rich" from many places, probably even from you! That's right—you may not think your child is listening, but conversations about a wealthy or struggling friend or neighbor, conversations about your financial state, or even jokes about winning the lottery can all prompt your child to ask this question.

In addition, young children talk to their friends about money and wealth. Don't believe me? Eavesdrop on some playground conversations between six- and seven-year-olds:

"Are you rich?" one may ask.

"I am! We have a sports car and a big, new TV."

"I am too. My dad works in the city at a really big office, and he said he makes so much money—that's why we can go on a cruise for vacation."

End of conversation.

How much of it is real? How much of it is made up to impress each other? It's hard to know, unless you're the parent of the child, but the conversation certainly triggers the question, doesn't it?

Kids also learn about being rich from TV. Ask yourself this question: do you monitor your child's TV viewing well enough to know that she is watching shows that don't project the message that great wealth is the only important aspect necessary to achieve happiness?

The older your child becomes, the more difficult it is to control TV viewing. What's more, a younger kid tends to watch whatever her older sibling is watching, which is almost always not age-appropriate for her (or sometimes for her older sibling either).

Whether or not you are rich, what response to this question is best for your child's emotional well-being?

The Best Way to Respond

Keep in mind that a child in this age range, even at the oldest end of it, doesn't need a detailed response. She needs a response that helps her to understand that being rich is not—at this point in her life—something about which she needs to worry. Furthermore, financial wealth is subjective. One may have five hundred thousand dollars and feel wealthy, while someone else may have ten million and feel poor. Last, wealth can, and should, also be measured in nonmonetary terms. One can be rich in love and friendship, rich in creativity, and rich in intelligence. These are different types of wealth that you can teach your child about—the younger the better!

Therefore, in responding to this question, a yes or no answer should be avoided. Even if your ego would love to simply yell out "Yes, we're rich—go and tell the world!" it is not in your child's best interest to have such information. Instead, a response similar to the following one is more beneficial to your child: "We are very rich in love and in family. We are rich with enough food and other comforts that give us what we need. We are rich with strong bodies and smart brains so that we can make sure that we can go to work and school to get even smarter and to make enough money to take care of our family. We are rich enough for us, and we don't compare our family to other families because every family is different and it's not a competition."

#37: IS THEIR HOUSE BIGGER THAN OUR HOUSE?

I guess I'm wrong—it is a competition!

Cynthia explained that her son Austen is very concerned with the size of people's homes: "When Austen (age 6½) goes to a friend's house for the first time, and sometimes when we're just passing a house, he will ask me if their house is bigger than ours. I don't know why this is so important to him."

There are several reasons your child may ask this question, but what is most important is the way you respond to it.

Uncovering the Meaning

It is possible that your child is asking this question in the same vein as Question #36—because he realizes that the size of a house may correlate with how "rich" someone is. However, it is improbable that a child in this age group will make that connection—except perhaps at the very oldest end of the age range.

It is more likely that your child is comparing house sizes out of sheer interest. Kids this age enjoy comparing and contrasting sizes and shapes—it is a cognitive task they are practicing and mastering; the more they do it, the better they get at it.

However, if you think that your child is asking about wealth and then respond accordingly, you could reinforce a negative stereotype without even realizing it. In fact, even if your child is comparing for that reason, it is far better to diffuse the comparison with a response that reflects a healthier viewpoint.

The Best Way to Respond

Your response should help your child see that homes come in all shapes and sizes, as do people. We should appreciate the beauty of every different type of home as we appreciate the beauty of people who live in them. A great response may be a variation of the following: "Yes, that house is bigger than our house—it's a very pretty house. And our house is bigger than that house over there. Isn't it interesting how many different size and shape houses there are in the world? And look how many different color houses there are too! Can you count the different colors? I also see so many different trees and flowers in front of the houses, and some houses are apartments—that's even more different, wow! Isn't it amazing how different houses can be? Also, look how many different kinds of people live in the different homes. Maybe when we go home we can draw a picture of lots of different kinds of homes and people, using as many different crayons as we can to show all the differences. We live in such a colorful world!"

8

Growing Up

It's hard to believe how fast a child grows up! It seems like with each passing day he becomes smarter and savvier about the ways of the world. But at the same time, each question your preschool- or early-elementary-age child asks reminds you that he is still as sweet and innocent as ever. These questions are the moments that you want to write in your memory book and keep forever! The questions in this chapter in particular are the ones that truly tug at your heart, make you giggle, and cause you to want to wrap your child into a gigantic snuggle. They are also the ones that may leave you utterly stumped for a good answer. But don't worry, I'll help you out with that, so let's get going.

#38: IS SANTA CLAUS/THE TOOTH FAIRY REAL?

Susanna, mother of Kim (age 5) and Jaime (age 8), explains a dilemma faced by many parents. "Jaime doesn't believe in the Tooth Fairy any more, but Kimmy still does. I keep telling Jaime not to say anything to Kim. Although it is funny that *both* girls still believe in Santa! I guess when you want to believe, you do!"

This is one of those painfully tough questions faced by parents in almost every home in one form or another. Why do kids believe in these magical fantasies? Why do we adults perpetuate them? Most importantly, should you eventually tell your child the cold, hard truth, or is it okay to let them keep believing? And the really tough one: if you should tell them, then when?

Uncovering the Meaning

Beginning in nursery school, but really peaking in preschool and kindergarten, a child's mind is open to the world of fantasy and pretend play. It is during this time that we see her deeply engaged in made-up games, sometimes alone, sometimes with friends (real and imaginary). This is a normal and healthy part of development, and it really helps a child to exercise her social and emotional "muscles." She will pretend to be a teacher, a firefighter, or a storekeeper. She is completely open to believing that Santa or the Tooth Fairy is real.

As your child moves into the early and later elementary grades, her thoughts become more pragmatic and less fantasy-based. You observe her play become more anchored in reality (board games, sports) and less motivated by make-believe. At the same time, she begins questioning those concepts that seem less than airtight ("How does the Tooth Fairy know that I lost my tooth, and how does she carry it away?" "How does Santa get to every child's house in one night, and how does he know what I wanted?").

However, at the same time, you still observe a yearning to believe. I know ten- and twelve-year-olds who still truly believe in the Tooth Fairy. And why not? We live in a world of harsh realities, so why not hang on to a little fantasy?

So what is the best way to respond to this question? Should you be truthful? Should you lie and risk your child finding out?

The Best Way to Respond

Kids are smart! In many cases a child won't ask this question if she doesn't want to know the answer. For example, if you have never been approached with this question, it is probably not because your child is less sophisticated than another child, but because she isn't yet ready to hear a response she might not like. In most situations with children this age, I recommend that when your child asks you this question, you respond by saying, "What do you think?" If your child tells you she thinks that Santa is real, I suggest you continue supporting this fantasy.

If she's ready to let it go, ask her why. She will be happy to tell you, and then you can validate her feelings. Of course, if she has decided not to believe because an older sibling has convinced her not to, don't be surprised if by tomorrow she believes again, because she wasn't truly ready to stop believing yet anyway. It is also perfectly acceptable to tell an older sibling not to spoil the fantasy for a younger sibling. In fact, some families I know have strict rules about this, and older siblings are told that they will be punished if they ruin it for a younger child who is still a "believer."

It's also okay to tell your child a variation of the following: "It's absolutely okay to know that Santa (or the Tooth Fairy) isn't real, but still keep pretending he is, because you enjoy being excited about it." By doing this you give your child permission to let go of the fantasy, which she may not believe in anymore, without letting go of the associated fun or goodies.

In our home, the Tooth Fairy doesn't come unless you believe in her—even my thirteen- and fifteen-year-old write her notes when they occasionally lose a molar. They don't want to risk that their tooth might still be there in the morning! I'm sure they don't really believe, but they are more than happy to play along with the game—perhaps for our benefit. My eleven-year-old, on the other hand, seems to truly believe in the Tooth Fairy. And I don't blame her—she has a loving and generous Tooth Fairy who not only leaves her gifts but sweet, personalized notes as well. She keeps every one of them in a box under her bed. I always fall asleep too early to catch sight of her Tooth Fairy—I wonder who it could be?

#39: IF I EAT MY CEREAL, WILL I BE A GOOD SOCCER PLAYER?

"Gotta love TV commercials!" said Candy, mom of Bethany (age 10), Jacob (age 7), and Heather (age 6) when she sent me this question. She is absolutely right. I don't want to pick on any one kind of food. It is fair to say that I received this question in a variety of formats from many different parents reflecting their frustration that their young children believe that all sorts of high-sugar, high-fat, or high-calorie products are going to help them achieve miraculous feats in their lives. Why is this? And what is there to be done about it?

Uncovering the Meaning

Preschool- and early-elementary-age children are very impressionable. Advertisers for food products know this, which is why they gear their advertising toward children beginning as young as nursery-school age. They know that a young child holds a mighty influence over his parents and that he will nag and beg until Mom or Dad purchases a widely advertised product that seems to hold miraculous qualities. Perhaps it makes you kick a ball further or helps you jump higher, it might make you happier or make kids like you better, or it could even somehow cause your world to seem more colorful and bright. Amazing!

There has historically been little care for ethics in the advertising world, and young children have always been the food companies' biggest victims because they do not yet have the cognitive capacity to differentiate between what is real in an advertisement and what is hype. Of course this holds true for advertising in the nonfood world as well. But when it comes to food, your child's health is at risk.

If you've read my book *Dr. Susan's Fit and Fun Family Action Plan*, you're already well educated about the many ways that children can become victims of media advertising. For example, did you know that preschool- and early-elementary-age children see one commercial for every five minutes of TV on weekend mornings, and that over 80 percent of foods advertised during TV shows targeted at kids are for fast food, snack foods, and sweets? As you can see from this question, the advertising is so cleverly delivered that it makes kids believe that the super-sweet cereal being advertised is going to make them more athletic.

That being said, some of the major food corporations (due to immense pressure from watchdog organizations) have joined a voluntary, self-regulating program called the Children's Food and Beverage Advertising Initiative. Members of the initiative (which is an arm of the Better Business Bureau, and it is the BBB that monitors the members' commitment to their pledges) agree to redirect their advertising and marketing dollars toward encouraging children to make healthier food choices. Specifically all companies have agreed to advertise and market only healthy foods to audiences of children that are primarily under twelve years old, and some companies have agreed to not advertise at all to audiences under six years old. This includes TV, radio, print, Internet, use of licensed characters, product placement, and in-school advertising. In addition, these companies pledge to agree to offer healthier choices for consumers (lower calories, sugar, fat, and sodium). The companies that have signed on to the pledge have already made some impressive and substantial initial changes to the way they market and advertise foods, as well as to some of the actual foods that they produce in order to make them healthier, and should be commended. These companies include Burger King, Cadbury Adams, Campbell Soup, Coca-Cola, ConAgra Foods, Dannon, General Mills, Hershey, Kellogg, Kraft

Foods, Mars, McDonald's, Nestlé, Pepsi, and Unilever. Each company's pledge is unique and may be viewed at www.us.bbb.org/advertisers4healthykids.

I would like to point out a couple of issues of which you should be aware. First, the members of the initiative have developed and are marketing foods to kids that by some standards are considered "better for you." This does not necessarily mean they are completely *good for you*. Next, just because these companies are producing some foods that are now somewhat healthier than they had been before the initiative, not every product that these companies produce falls into this category. They still carry products that are not healthy for your child, so don't assume that just because a company has joined this initiative, that every food or beverage it sells is healthy—or even healthier than before. And last, not all food companies have joined the initiative; there are still plenty of powerful media out there that can impact on your child's relationship with food.

Therefore, as impressive as this pledge is, it is still your job to make sure that your child understands the relationship between food and the media. This includes the way foods are marketed in the supermarket (using licensed characters), the way advertising makes foods seem so desirable, and the way product placement is used. Product placement is when a specific brand of a product is placed in a TV show or movie that your child watches, making them want to have that product.

The way you answer this question and others like it will go a long way to teaching your child about these relationships.

The Best Way to Respond

Responding to this question requires you to draw a direct relationship between advertising and the food your child desires. A child this young will not understand a more subtle approach. Try a variation of the following: "You've probably seen advertisements on TV for your favorite cereal, and the kids were playing soccer and it was really cool! I bet that seeing all these ads is what is making you think that eating *their* cereal will make you a better soccer player. Well, guess what? That's what the makers of the cereal want you to think. The truth is that you will get good at playing soccer if you eat healthy food and, most importantly, if you practice soccer." Go on to give your child another example of how advertising works so he will begin to really understand it. Then when you see examples of it on TV or anywhere else, point them out.

When you are in the supermarket, talk to your child about product placement. Explain how connecting his or her favorite food or candy with a brand-new movie makes it seem more desirable. If you think that your child is too young to start learning these lessons, think again. You can start to have these kinds of conversations with a child as young as six, and by second grade your child will be educating other kids about how licensed characters are really just a way to get parents to buy more junk food.

#40: WHEN WILL I BE GROWN UP?
(OR: WHEN WILL I BE OLD ENOUGH TO WATCH A PG MOVIE/SIT IN THE FRONT SEAT?)

Some young children, especially those with older siblings, can't wait to be more grown up. They so badly want all the privileges that accompany being a big kid, and they become indignant when faced with the limitations of their young age.

Mae's (5½) mother, Lydia, shared Mae's frequent exasperation with her status in life as a first-grader. "Mae is constantly asking me when she'll be grown up. She wants to be able to ride bikes with the big kids, watch big-kid TV shows, and stay up later. She says it is taking so long and that it's 'not fair' that her older sister and brother get to do so much more than her. I explain to her that when she's older she'll get to do everything, but she wants to do it all right now."

Lydia is not alone. Thousands of parents everywhere have young children just like Mae—constantly striving to be older. What is this all about and what should you do about it?

Uncovering the Meaning

This type of question can be so annoying to you that you might be wondering why I didn't put it in Chapter One, "Nag, Nag, Nag." However, the truth is that while you may sometimes experience it as nagging, this question really reflects your child's drive to continue moving forward as she grows and changes. A child who is completely complacent—with no interest in pushing the limits at all to try new, more challenging experiences—will not grow emotionally and developmentally. Asking you when she will be grown up is the way your child expresses her desire to achieve more, learn more, and become more! You should celebrate your child's aspiration to embrace her future while at the same time you recognize that a child in the preschool and early elementary years needs clear and specific boundaries. While she may want to be grown up and to do all the things that older kids do, it is not in her best interest for you to facilitate this simply because it is her desire. Rather, it is much more important for you to weather the storm of her frustration; respond to her questions in a manner that helps her understand that she is not yet old enough to do the things that older children do.

Teaching your child this now sets the stage for the future. There will be countless times, as your child matures, when she will want to be able to do things that you do not believe she is ready to do. As her parent, it is your right to place limits on what you permit your child to experience, as you see fit. We will explore this parenting concept in greater detail in *The Top 50 Questions Kids Ask (3rd through 5th Grade)*, because this is when your child will really begin pushing you to let her grow up—and way too fast!

The Best Way to Respond

Your response should be clear and a variation of the following: "You will be grown up when you are older. There is no hurry to grow up. But guess what? You are learning so many new things all the time, and I am so proud of you. You are learning to read and to add and subtract. You are making new friends and getting really good at baseball. When you are older you will be able to do the things that older kids do, I promise. But there are lots of things that you can do that babies and toddlers can't do. So you just have to be patient."

I strongly encourage you to stick to your guns and *not* allow your child to engage in experiences that are too advanced for her, either because she is asking (begging), or because you have older children and she gets to go along with them. Young children can be emotionally damaged by exposure to information or experiences that is not appropriate for them. The following suggestions are guidelines to help you:

- Screen *all* media, including TV, movies (big screen and home), books, magazines, computer games, and music before allowing your young child access to them. If you need help with this

I strongly recommend Common Sense Media (CommonSenseMedia.org), a nonprofit organization dedicated to helping parents gain the knowledge and information necessary to make the best media decisions for their children. Ratings are there for a reason—young children should not be exposed to mature concepts, violence, or sex.

- Do not give in to the urge to leave your young child alone, no matter for short a time or how much she begs that she is old enough (in the car, in the house, in a supermarket aisle—*anywhere*!).

- Most young children aren't emotionally mature enough for scary events like haunted houses, but won't admit it if all the older kids are going. They will say they are fine, but be terrified afterward, and you'll be stuck dealing with the nightmares. Therefore, you need to make the decision for your child—even if she begs to go.

- Your young child needs enough sleep, so don't let her persuade you that she is grown up enough to stay up later. If you are not convinced, read Chapter Three, Question #13, "Can I stay up later?"

- Resist the urge to allow your young child to sit in the front seat of the car. You might be tired of the nagging, but nagging is better than a dead or badly injured child. Airbags can cause severe head trauma to young children, as can a head-on collision. Your child is not grown up enough for the front seat until she reaches the age that it is allowed by law. Explain this clearly. Oh, and no one is too old for seat belts—hopefully you are role-modeling this for your child.

#41: WHERE DO BABIES COME FROM? (OR: DID I COME OUT OF YOUR BELLY BUTTON? DID A STORK BRING ME TO YOU? HOW DID I GET BORN?)

Tammy admits to being slightly panicked when Kurt (age 5) sprang this question on her. She explained, "But, just as I was about to stumble through a response to Kurt, the baby began to cry, so both he and I were distracted. Whew! But I'm not sure what I will say next time he asks."

Of course, this (and the variations of it) was one of the top questions parents sent me. Just about every parent is faced with this question at one time or another and many dread it. You want to be able to respond to it in a relaxed way, but you're just not sure exactly what to say, how much to explain, and what your child really wants to hear.

Uncovering the Meaning

Perhaps it's your own pregnancy, or the pregnancy of a relative or a friend's parent that triggers your child's curiosity, or maybe it's a book he read in school. It may even be a pregnant animal. But one way or another, your child will eventually ask the dreaded question—and in all likelihood it will be before he exits the second grade, so if it hasn't happened yet, read this section with great care.

To begin, your child's developmental level changes vastly as he progresses through preschool into the early elementary grades, which is why you may hear this question over and over again. I'm sure you're thrilled to know that! In general, the question of a three- or four-year-old (and the response he expects) will be very different from that of a six- or seven-year-old. It is therefore important to be sure that you know exactly what your child is really asking you.

My friend's five-year-old son once asked her "Where did I come from?" She braced herself and launched into a complete and admirable explanation about conception. When she was done, she breathed a satisfied sigh of relief. "But I thought I was born in Brooklyn," said her son, now slightly overloaded with more information than he had anticipated receiving!

A now-famous story that I tell about my son (then seven, now sixteen) when he asked me the dreaded "Where do babies come from?" question is that, as I began to tell him the details, he put his palm up to my face.

"STOP!" He demanded. "I've heard this once from my friend, and I don't want to hear it again!" Apparently, I was offering much more information than he really wanted at that moment—or maybe he simply wanted confirmation that the weird story his friend had told him about babies was true! I guess even child psychologists don't get it right every time!

The Best Way to Respond

When you decide that your child does want to know the biology of where babies come from, you need to be ready for the conversation. The following tips will prepare you, so you don't have to live in fear for the next several years:

- Use age-appropriate language that your child understands.
- Very young children will be satisfied with knowing that "a tiny egg grows inside a special part of a mommy's body and becomes a baby."
- Older children (around six or seven years old or older depending on your child) can be told that "when a mommy and daddy love each other very much they lay very close together and they make a baby."
- If you feel compelled to be very specific, say, "A mommy has a vagina, and a daddy has a penis. The daddy puts his penis in the mommy's vagina and that can make a baby." Expect your child to be shocked or say, "Eeewww, that's disgusting!"
- If you have an adopted child, be sure to include the concept of adoption in your discussion of "where babies come from."
- If necessary (but only *if*) you can also explain about a C-section.

- No matter how awkward you feel, resist the urge to talk about storks, seeds, or other fictitious ways babies might arrive.
- Don't say that the baby grows in the mommy's belly or tummy because your child may worry that he (or she) could spontaneously become pregnant. Explain that the baby grows in a special place inside the mommy, near the tummy, that only mommies and grown-up girls have.
- If the conversation is just too difficult for you, it is fine to use a "where do babies come from" book to help you out—it does *not* make you a bad parent!

#42: WHY DOES HE HAVE A PENIS AND I DON'T?
(OR: WHY DOESN'T SHE HAVE ONE TOO?)

Marguerite was still giggling when she reported this story to me, "I had to laugh when Ashley (age 4) asked me why her brother Trevor (age 7) has a penis and she doesn't. Penis envy? Is that actually real?"

Penis envy has, for the most part, been debunked as a true psychological syndrome. Interestingly the roots of this theory can be found in Sigmund Freud's Oedipal complex, which we looked at in Chapter Six, "Step-by-Step Separation." While some aspects of the Oedipal complex seem to have stood the test of time (see

Question #32, "Can I marry you when I'm grown up?"), despite Freud's monumentally male-chauvinist view of the world, penis envy is definitely not one of them. Why then, does your child ask this question?

Uncovering the Meaning

Beginning around three years old, it is normal for your child to become interested in other people's bodies. She will show a fascination with your body as well as the bodies of her peers. A completely different developmental milestone that your child will reach around this age is the beginning ability to differentiate between "same" and "different" items. She will enjoy playing games in which she has to notice the difference between items. You know the catchy song and game from the *Sesame Street* TV show, "One of These Things (Is Not Like the Others)"? The reason it appeals to young children is specifically because they are newly interested in noticing differences! This newfound ability to notice differences is the main reason your child is so fascinated with the difference in genitalia between girls and boys (and men and women).

Both girls and boys will wonder why a boy has a penis and a girl does not. However, that doesn't mean a girl experiences herself as deficit in any way. In fact most girls will say "eeww" if you ask them whether they would prefer to have a penis—and vice versa for boys.

Of course, your child may pretend or "try out" being the opposite sex in play—she may dress like her brother or a friend who is a boy, or even experiment with urinating standing up to see what it feels like. This is not something to worry about as long as it is temporary.

That being said, it is around this age that *unusual* instances of Gender Identity Disorder (GID) might manifest. GID is diagnosed when children feel very strongly that they do not want to be their own gender *and* that they do want to be the other gender. Sometimes GID lasts into adolescence and adulthood, and some kids with GID grow up to be homosexual.

If your child displays any of the following symptoms for more than a passing time, it is important to seek experienced professional help for yourself and your child. Be aware that many professionals may be interested in working with you, because you and your child may be a fascinating family for them to see, but this does not mean they will be able to provide you with the support and guidance you need.

A child with GID will

- want to dress in real (if available) or dress-up clothes of the opposite sex, and will reject efforts to dress him or her in gender-consistent clothes (like a dress for a girl)
- want to look like the opposite gender (a girl will want to keep her hair short, a boy may want to grow his long)
- talk about wanting to be the opposite sex or might insist that he or she is the opposite sex

- believe that when she or he grows up she or he will become an adult of the opposite sex (e.g., a girl might say, "When I grow up I'm going to be a daddy")
- reject his or her genitalia (e.g., a boy might say, "I hate my penis")
- want to play primarily with peers of the opposite sex and only with games/toys identified with the opposite sex (children that will later grow up to be gay, but not have GID, may also do this)

In the vast majority of instances, GID has nothing to do with your child's interest in anatomy of the opposite gender, so what is the best way to respond?

The Best Way to Respond

When you are asked this question it is most important to keep a straight face. Remember that for your child, this is serious business—she is trying to understand why people are so different from each other.

Your goal is to use this question as an opportunity to do two things:

1. Use this as a first chance to let your child know she can talk to you about *any* topic—even when it includes sexual body parts—and make sure she realizes that you won't become embarrassed or jittery. This will set the stage for later. If your child senses that you are uncomfortable, it is less likely that she will come to you in the future with her intimate questions.

2. Provide a response that answers the question clearly, but does not overload your child with information. Start small. Use proper words for body parts—please! For example, explain by saying, "Boys and girls are different because a girl eventually becomes a woman and she can have a baby. Having a vagina is part of having a baby. A man doesn't have babies so he doesn't need a vagina, so he has a penis." This will more than suffice for a three- to five-year-old, possibly even an older child. If your child keeps asking questions, you can add, "Having a penis lets a daddy help a mommy make a baby when the mommy and daddy lay very close to each other and they want to make a baby." We are now getting into the "Where do babies come from?" category, so you may want to reread Question #41 to brush up on *that* question.

#43: WHY DO SOME PEOPLE HAVE BROWN (OR WHITE) SKIN?
(OR: WHY ARE SOME PEOPLE FAT AND SOME PEOPLE THIN? WHY DOES THAT PERSON HAVE DIFFERENT EYES?)

Like Question #42, this one also indicates that your child is beginning to become observant and notice differences between people. Carolina, the mother of very chatty twins Derek and Dawson (age 6), explained that her twins recently began asking her about the color of people's skin. "I'm not sure what to tell them," she explained. "It seems so complicated. And sometimes they ask me other questions about people—in front of the people—that are embarrassing. They ask me things like, 'How come some people have white skin and some people have brown skin?' which is an okay question. Or how about, 'Why are some people fat and some aren't?' right in front of someone who is overweight. Or another embarrassing one: 'How come some people have such *big* hair and other people's hair is normal?' as we're standing next to a woman whose hair is a huge pile of uncontrolled frizz."

So, how do you negotiate your child's curiosity about the world in a way that isn't a liability to you?

Uncovering the Meaning

A young child begins with a completely clean, unbiased view of other people. When he asks you this question, it is out of pure curiosity, and nothing more.

As Carolina mentioned, sometimes your child may ask you this or a similar question, in a way that could embarrass you. Recognize that it is not your child's intention to embarrass you. Rather, he doesn't yet have the social savvy to recognize that certain questions are better whispered. It is your job to help your child learn how to ask questions in a way that is more socially aware, without making him feel that he can't be curious and open-minded.

The Best Way to Respond

If you want to help your child to remain unbiased and accepting of all people as equals (and I hope that you do), then recognize that his understanding at this age of why his skin is a different color from someone else's skin is largely a result of what you tell him. This is a critical time to begin teaching your child about respecting, tolerating, and appreciating the differences between people. Your response should therefore be a variation of the following: "Nature (or God) makes all beautiful things in lots of different colors—flowers, trees, rocks, and even people! It is great that people come in so many different colors because it makes the world more interesting and fun. People are different in lots of other ways too—you like chocolate ice cream, but I like strawberry. You like playing with cars, but your friend Casey likes blocks more. We still love each other and are friends with each other even though we are different. Well, it's the same with skin."

When your child asks a question at a time or in a manner that may be embarrassing to you or inadvertently hurtful to someone else, it is important to help him understand this, rather than simply accept it as "cute." This is the only way he will begin to recognize this behavior and correct it. However, it is also important to keep in mind that this is a learning process for your child.

Don't allow your own embarrassment to make you overly angry with your child. In this situation, before responding to your child's question, you first need to discuss with him the way his question may have affected the other person—do so quietly and gently. If necessary, help him to apologize to the person he embarrassed, or if he is too shy or upset, apologize for him so he can see you role-modeling socially appropriate behavior. You should explain that even though he didn't realize it, certain questions might hurt people's feelings, and that sometimes it is a good idea to whisper a question if you're not sure. Questions about peoples' bodies, hair, clothes, or behavior are usually the ones you have to ask quietly. This is probably a lesson you will have to remind him of many times before it sinks in.

#44: WHERE WAS I WHEN MY (OLDER) BROTHER/SISTER WAS BORN?
(OR: WHY AREN'T I IN YOUR WEDDING VIDEO? WAS I BORN THEN [REFERRING TO A TIME LONG BEFORE HE WAS BORN]? WAS I IN YOUR TUMMY WHEN THAT HAPPENED? WAS MY LITTLE BROTHER IN YOUR TUMMY, OR WAS HE IN MY TUMMY? WHEN WILL I BE IN THE SAME GRADE AS MY BROTHER?)

"Marisol (age 4) gets so confused," laughed her father, Diego. "She always asks questions like, 'Daddy, where was I when Luci (age 7) was a baby?' No matter how many times I explain it to her, she doesn't get it!"

It is very common for a young child to feel confused by the sequence of events in her life, and who was where, and when. Something that seems so logical to an adult may make no sense to a young child. Why is this, and how can you help your child get a better grasp on the events in her life—as well as those events *not* actually in her life, so she is less frustrated and confused?

Uncovering the Meaning

Your child learns the concept of time and the sequence of events gradually as she grows up. Keep in mind that just as with every other skill, every child learns about time and sequence at her own rate, and there is no right or wrong time to get it right.

Before three years old, your child understands very little about time and routine. She will then begin to grasp current sequences in her everyday life—her own daily routine, that Mommy comes home just before bath time, and that bedtime is after dinner. Attending school—which is all about sequence and routine—helps teach and reinforce this skill.

A child of three or four has very little concept of time beyond the here and now, which is why consequences for negative behavior are meaningless if they are not immediate (two days later, your four-year-old will have forgotten why she can't watch TV). Over the next couple of years, your child will become better able to recognize and appreciate sequences that are further into the future, like birthdays and holidays, but the distant past remains somewhat murky.

As your child moves through the early elementary grades, her ability to understand the past will begin to improve, especially with your help. By seven or eight years old, she should have a fairly good understanding of the sequence of events in her life as they really happened, and if she doesn't, she should be able to grasp an explanation that teaches the sequence to her.

The Best Way to Respond

When your child asks you this question, you can assume that she is struggling not only with this particular question (or a similar one), but with the concept of the sequencing of life events in general.

One of the best ways to begin to help your child start to learn about sequencing is to give her a calendar. She will be most receptive to this idea beginning around five years old, although I know some four-year-olds who enjoy calendars. It doesn't have to be a fancy, expensive calendar—she will be thrilled with the free one that one of your local merchants gave you. Help her to mark all the important events in her life (birthdays of friends and family, her activities, days she goes to school, days she doesn't, activities she attends). If she can't read, pictures or stickers work well.

Another extremely effective method for teaching your child about the sequence of events in her life is to start telling her stories about her life and your life, beginning before she was born. Hearing the stories will not only fascinate and thrill her far more than a story in a picture book, it will teach her the true sequence of events as they occurred and help her to grasp how she fits in the picture. When she asks you this question, you can actually respond with a story that explains the sequence so she understands that she wasn't born until later.

Last, picture time lines, drawn while you are telling a story, can be very helpful for a young child. For example, as you are explaining how wonderful your wedding was, and that you came back and moved into your new home and then had a baby, you can draw pictures of each of these things one after the other. The visual order will help your child to grasp why she couldn't possibly have been in the wedding video. Remember though, that she still needs to have the cognitive capacity to understand this, which will come with time as she continues to grow up.

9

Just between You and Me

Young children don't yet have enough knowledge about the world to ask you too many really tough, personal questions, but that doesn't mean they won't ask you any. You definitely should be prepared for some awkward moments. In fact, your child may ask you questions that she doesn't even realize are personal and perhaps embarrassing. She's just asking what's on her mind. The manner in which you answer these questions is important, not only because you want to think about the information you divulge to your child, but also because she may share that information with others.

Young kids are notorious blabbermouths. Asking your child not to tell anyone what you told her is not a good idea. You might confuse her. You have probably told her that keeping secrets isn't good, so she won't understand why you are asking her to keep one. What's more, if she accidentally tells, she will feel bad or worry that you will be angry with her.

So, what are the most common personal questions that young kids ask? You are about to find out!

#45: HOW OLD ARE YOU?

"Jack (age 5) loves to ask me my age," offered his mother, Vanessa, speaking in a group of women, "especially when we're in public. It's not that I'm so embarrassed about it (forty-three), but I did have Jack when I was a bit older. Most of his friends' moms are around mid-thirties or even younger. I don't really feel like broadcasting my age, but when I don't tell him, he keeps badgering me!"

Erin, Lacey's (age 4½) mom, has a different dilemma. "Vanessa, I can understand how you feel. I also don't like to share my age when Lacey asks me at the top of her voice, but it's because I'm much *younger* than everyone else! I was twenty-two when I had Lacey, so most of the moms are ten years older than me. I worry that they'll judge me badly for having had a baby too young or for not being an experienced enough parent."

As you can see, if you feel uncomfortable with this question, you are not alone. For these and numerous other reasons, you may not be sure how to respond to this question in a way that makes you feel comfortable and still meets your child's need for information.

Uncovering the Meaning

In most instances, your child is asking your age simply because she is curious about how old you are compared to her, or compared to her teacher or another adult or older child. Perhaps she has been learning about numbers in school, and she is trying to gain some perspective. Or maybe someone's birthday is coming up (yours or someone else's) and that has piqued her interest in peoples' ages.

The truth is that for children younger than six, your age is meaningless. Even for an older child, it doesn't mean all that much. In fact, recently my fifteen-year-old was describing one of his teachers. Her age was somehow relevant to the discussion, "Well how old do you think she is?" I asked.

"Oh, I don't know. Really old."

"Well, about how old?"

"I dunno, she's going to have a baby soon..."

Well, okay then. That sure is old!

Even though your child may not have a real sense of what your age means, it doesn't mean you shouldn't give her an answer. Not responding, or saying you don't want to tell her, will frustrate her or make her even more curious. If you are comfortable telling your child your age, it's easy, but if you're not, then keep reading.

The Best Way to Respond

One of the most effective ways to respond to a very young child is to lie. Now, don't get upset. This is not a major lie, and remember that your child doesn't really have any concept of your age anyway. The key is to be consistent and outrageous so that other adults will realize that the number you gave is a joke. For example if you are forty, tell your child that you are twenty-one. If you are twenty-five, tell your child that you are eighteen or forty-five—whichever seems right to you. Your child will be satisfied, and you will not have to reveal your age.

Another fail-safe way to handle this is to ask your child how old she thinks you are, and then agree with whatever she says. Just don't be insulted if she says, "I think you're fifty-nine, Mommy!"

#46: CAN I SHOWER WITH YOU [OPPOSITE-SEX PARENT]? (OR: WHY WON'T YOU TAKE A BATH WITH ME?)

Nancy used to enjoy showering with her son Alec. But since Alec was about three and a half, she stopped. "I just don't feel comfortable anymore," explained Nancy, "but it has been a few months and Alec still asks me. Have I made the right decision? His dad still bathes with him. That's okay, right?"

This is one of the most controversial topics I have ever encountered. The range of opinions is enormous as to whether an opposite-sex parent should bathe with a child. In fact there is even debate among parents as to whether a parent of the same sex should be doing it. So what's the bottom line?

Uncovering the Meaning

Let's begin with one important point: although there are no hard and fast, right or wrong responses, we will discuss some psychological guidelines, which should help you respond in a way that is in the best interest of your child.

Much of your initial opinion, comfort level, and decision making about whether or not to bathe with your child, for how long to do it, and when to stop has its genesis in the way you were raised. You tend to either follow the same blueprint or do the opposite. This is why there are so many different opinions about the subject—each of us was raised so differently.

Up until age three or even slightly older, there is absolutely no reason for an opposite-sex parent to stop showering or bathing with a child, unless the parent feels discomfort or the child expresses discomfort. A child this age is beginning to form a sense of his own gender, but this does not mean he should not be exposed to the nudity of his parent of the opposite gender. In fact, as long as you are comfortable responding to questions about your body parts, this is the time to do it.

Beginning around four years old is a good time to stop showering or bathing with an opposite-sex child. Around this time your child may be developing Oedipal tendencies (see Chapter Six, Question #32) and bathing with him could be confusing and make it difficult for him to understand the appropriate boundaries in your relationship (of course this is true for both genders).

In addition, beginning at this age, a child needs to start to learn about keeping his own body private. *This is important for boys and for girls.* Of course your child doesn't have to keep his body private from you, but for a young child, boundaries are very blurred unless we adults help solidify them. Not bathing with an opposite-sex parent is a safe boundary to instill beginning in preschool. In addition, children also chat! Your child's teacher may not think it is "appropriate" that an opposite-sex parent still bathes with your child. Do you want the staff at school talking about you?

Furthermore, any time from four years old on—if you have not done so already—is a good time to teach your child to wash his own body (of course a little girl with long hair may need help with her hair for a while). Learning independence is very important and so is the idea that he should be the only one to touch his "private parts"—other than you if absolutely necessary.

The response for same-sex parents is, in my opinion, quite different. It is fine to continue bathing with your same-sex child for as long as you and he are comfortable (in fact, I highly recommend it). Your child will learn about what an adult body of his gender looks like close up, will have the chance to ask questions (which you must be prepared to answer!), and will have a chance to form an intimate bond with you, stripped of any "formalities."

Despite my recommendation, if you are not comfortable bathing or showering nude with your child past a certain age, then don't do it! Your child will pick up on your lack of comfort, and this could cause your child to feel shameful about his body. In addition, if your child doesn't want to bathe with you, you *must* respect his wishes. Allowing your child body privacy is very, very important at all times.

Don't forget that if you feel sad about the idea of not bathing with your child anymore, there is nothing wrong with putting on a bathing suit and jumping in the bath or shower.

Now that you understand the issues, what's the best way to respond to your child?

The Best Way to Respond

If you have reached the point when you no longer feel comfortable showering or bathing with your opposite-sex child, you will need to help your child make the shift too. When your child is young, this is not the type of question that requires a complex response. Your child will not understand that you are no longer showering with him for reasons of privacy. Rather, you can divert your child's attention, re-create the schedule, or make sure that you shower when your child is not around until he becomes accustomed to not showering with you. In addition, you need to make sure you do not shower with a younger sibling in front of him.

If your child is older (probably seven years or older), you may need to offer an explanation that should be a variation of the following: "From now on everyone is going to take their own showers (or baths). You're big enough to have privacy now when you take a shower and also to learn to do all the washing by yourself." Your child will feel proud about focusing on the independence part of it and will likely think little about the fact that he will no longer be bathing with you. If he asks if he can still do it once in a while, explain that now that he is big, he is going to shower/bathe by himself.

#47: WHY DO YOU WANT TO LOSE WEIGHT?

"I was a little shocked to hear my seven-year-old asking me this question!" remarked Miranda, whose daughter Michaela had been watching her eat salad for lunch that day. Miranda shouldn't be surprised, because research shows that on any given day, 45 percent of American women (and 25 percent of American men) are on a diet.

Her child observed her behavior and is trying to understand what it means.

For years, we have heard that we need to be careful about the way we talk to preteens and teens about weight loss and dieting. However, the truth is that a child's concern about these things—and the risk for her developing an eating disorder—can begin much younger than that. So what does this question mean, and are there better and worse ways to respond to it? You bet there are.

Uncovering the Meaning

When a young child asks you this question (or a similar one) it means that she has overheard you making a comment or having a conversation about wanting to lose weight. Now she is trying to understand and process that information.

A very young child (under five years) probably will not understand the concept of dieting or weight loss and won't pay attention to what you are eating or how much you are exercising. But beginning at about five or certainly six years old, your child—especially a girl—might begin to notice. She may think you are crazy to want to lose weight because she thinks you are perfect just the way you are.

On the other hand, she might start to copy you—telling people that she wants to lose weight or go on a diet. While she might not really know what this means or how to do it, this is not emotionally healthy behavior (even if she is overweight). In addition, if she sees you rejecting your body—especially if she thinks your body is fine just as it is—she may start to look for reasons to reject her own body too.

In general, it is in your child's best interest not to discuss dieting or weight loss in her presence. In addition, refrain from making self-critical comments in front of your child ("I hate my thighs," "I look so fat in this," "I've definitely gained weight"). If you are not overweight, it is *particularly* important for you to be self-reflective about your interest in weight loss. A child (especially a girl) whose mother is overly concerned with weight and body image (her own or her daughter's) is more likely to develop her own body image problem—which could lead to an eating disorder.

As you can probably tell by now, in order to reinforce a positive self-image for your child, you need to think carefully about the way you respond to this question.

The Best Way to Respond

You need to teach your child that a person should only decide to lose weight in a safe and medically supervised fashion (regardless of whether this is what you are actually practicing). Therefore, you may answer this question with a variation of the following: "I am losing some weight because my doctor told me that it would be healthier for me." In addition, your child needs to know that it is *not* healthy for a child to diet. You can therefore add, "Children don't lose weight in the same way as adults. Children eat healthy foods and run around and ride bikes. That's how kids keep healthy. Kids don't go on diets, and they don't lose weight unless their doctors or parents tell them they need to."

#48: WHAT ARE YOU GOING TO BE WHEN YOU GROW UP?

Shannon and Jeremy love answering this question when Ethan (age 5) asks them. Jeremy kids around with Ethan. "Each time we give him a different answer! Last week I told him I wanted to be an architect when I grow up. 'Why?' he said. 'You're already an architect.'"

It seems like such a silly question, but to your child it is quite serious. It represents his way of asking you for some guidance as to how he should begin looking at his future—remember you are his most important role model. So how do you give him what he's looking for? It's not that difficult.

Uncovering the Meaning

To some degree, this question reflects your child's difficulty with understanding the concept of time and sequence (see Chapter Eight, Question #44).

However, in the greater psychological world, your

child is just beginning to think about what he would like to be when he grows up. Of course, he will try out a great many different roles before he settles on one. This is an exciting and normal part of development. In fact, before he is ten years old he will probably have insisted, at least ten times, that he has found the perfect job for himself—whether it be professional ball player, celebrity chef, deep sea fisherman, or school teacher! A few kids will latch onto the idea of one career (often a professional athlete) and stick with it for a long time. You may be concerned that your child will never change his mind. Don't worry, he will.

By asking you this question, your child is actually trying to get some ideas that will help to shape his identity as he grows up. Since you are his greatest role model, he values the ideas and choices that you make and might add them to his possible repertoire of ideas.

Since you are a great influence on your child, the way you offer ideas is important—not in terms of an ultimate career choice of course (he is way too young for that), but in terms of helping him develop into an open-minded, confident, and creative individual.

The Best Way to Respond

This question gives you a fantastic opportunity to show your child that he has the whole world ahead of him, with so many choices and chances, as long as he works hard. Your response might sound similar to the following: "When I grow up I'm going to work really, really hard, but I'm not sure yet what I'm going to be. I might be a writer because I love to write, and I might be a psychologist because I love to help people. I think I could even be a teacher. There are so many choices. But I'm not going to decide yet because I want to keep thinking about it. What do you think you want to be? What are the things you love the most?"

Of course it's fine to give your child specific ideas of what you might like to be when you "grow up" (like Jeremy and Shannon do), but you might want to add, "When you grow up you don't have to be the same things as me, you can choose your own ideas."

#49: WHEN YOU HAVE A BABY, DO YOU HAVE TO GET MARRIED?

"Rachel (age 8) seemed to have the order slightly mixed up!" said her mother, Dana. "But when I tried to explain it to her, she wanted nothing to do with it! 'I'm not getting married,' she said. 'Boys are gross! But babies are cute!' And that was the end of that conversation."

Clearly, Rachel is missing a couple of steps here when it comes to having a baby and boys being gross, but let's put that aside for now. It is not all that unusual for a little girl to focus on the order in which these two events take place. This, like some of the other questions we have discussed, has to do with the fact that she doesn't yet have a good grasp on time lines. Of course, perhaps she has had a life experience that includes observing a woman who has a baby without getting married. Or maybe she knows someone who is single with a small child, and she doesn't know whether the woman was married at some point.

We live in a time when the guaranteed order of marriage, pregnancy, and birth is not clear-cut. In fact, marriage doesn't even occur every time. On many different levels, this is a tough one.

Uncovering the Meaning

You may find that your child is very interested in the idea of marriage—some little girls are, because they picture it much like "playing house" and they want it all: the house, the marriage, and the baby!

However, when a very young child asks this question, it is typically because, like Rachel, she is currently not thrilled about the concept of marriage ("boys are gross"), but she would be happy to have a cute, snuggly baby— sort of like her baby doll. She is not very focused on the details or mechanics. Rather, it is the end result that interests her. You need to keep in mind that this question represents a temporary phase and nothing more.

An older child (seven or eight) may be asking because she has observed a woman who has had a baby out of wedlock. Perhaps she knows a pregnant teenager or a friend of the family. She may even have seen an unmarried mother on television. Since a recent government survey indicates that nearly four out of ten pregnancies in the United States are out of wedlock (taking into account a *drop* in teen pregnancy), it's not surprising that your child might be asking this question.

However, although there are varying opinions as to whether it is good or bad to have a baby while single, research shows that it is not in a woman's or her child's best interest to do so. Single mothers are five times more likely than those who are married to live below the poverty line. Children in single-mother families are more likely to have psychological difficulties, and they are more likely to drop out of school. Therefore, the way you respond to this question should be carefully thought out, even when your child is young, because your initial response sets the stage for how you can talk to her about this topic on a going-forward basis. In addition, although it is less likely that your son will ask you this question, it is not a bad topic to discuss with him when he is a little older.

The Best Way to Respond

Tell your child a variation of the following: "You don't have to worry about it too much right now, but the order in which it works is that *first* you get married and *then* you have a baby! You may not feel like getting married now because you are still a little girl, and you are not supposed to like boys yet. But when you are older, you might change your mind. Until then you can play with your dolls and pretend they are babies. But the rule is marriage first and baby second—it's just a rule, I didn't make it up!"

There will be plenty of time to debate the pros and cons of a woman having a baby because her biological clock is running out and she still hasn't found a husband. This isn't the time for that!

#50: WHEN YOU GREW UP, DID YOU WANT TO BE A MOMMY/DADDY?

Well, did you?

When I was a teenager, I couldn't wait to be a mother. But not every woman I know feels that way. When Logan (age 5) asked his mother, Kimberly, this question, she was a little taken aback. "The truth is I didn't really want to be a mother until after I was married. But I didn't know what to tell Logan. I thought it might hurt his feelings if I told him the truth, so I just changed the subject."

What is your child really wondering about when he asks this question? And what's the best way to handle it—is a little white lie okay?

Uncovering the Meaning

From your child's perspective, this is a very sweet question. It is similar to Question #48, "What are you going to be when you grow up?" because it is your child's way of trying to understand how you got from being a child just like him, to being a parent.

How did it happen? Was there something magical that occurred inside you that made you realize that you wanted to be a mom or dad? Will it ever happen to him? For some parents, this may feel like a trick question because the decision to have a child was complicated or because their child was unplanned (they had no intention of becoming a parent at all or not at that time). In this case, you may not be at all sure how to respond to your child.

The bottom line is that, if you can't truthfully answer this question with, "Yes, I've always wanted to be a parent," then what should you say?

The Best Way to Respond

Your child doesn't have a preconceived idea about how you should respond. Nor does he expect you to have wanted to be a parent since you were his age. On the other hand, if deciding to become a parent was a difficult process for you, or if being a parent was or still is not easy, then being brutally honest is not a good idea.

Despite how you may feel, your response needs to take into account what is best for your child—it should make him feel loved. It is fine to explain that arriving at the decision to have a child was a process for you, rather than a quick decision, but that once you made the decision, you were absolutely sure it was the right one. You need to say this even if it is not entirely true because *your child needs to think and feel that you love being a parent*. You will want to leave out any parts that involve your pregnancy being unplanned. Your response should sound something like this: "When I was a little girl, I wasn't sure if I wanted to be a mom. I wasn't even sure yet when I was a teenager. But when I was a bit older and I met your dad, I started to know that I wanted to be a mom. I became more and more sure. And then I had you and your sister, and it was the best decision I ever made! I love being a mom, and you are the best kids that any mom could ever ask for. Even on the days when we argue, or the days that we are grumpy or sad, being a parent makes me happy inside and out!"

One Last Question

Congratulations! I now consider you an expert on the questions of young children! After reading this book, I'm sure that you realize you can learn a lot from your child by paying attention to his questions.

But this last question is for you.

Will you truly make an effort to apply what you've learned in these pages?

I hope that you do. Your child's questions are a window to his soul. When you pay close attention to each question, and you do not dismiss it as trivial, there is so much to learn about your child and so much more for you to teach him.

We live rushed lives in a busy world. It is easy to read and forget, to promise that you will make changes and then forget to prioritize those changes.

I ask you to remember that you have only one childhood with your child, one set of questions, and only one chance to answer those questions the right way. Don't blink, because before you know it, your first grader will be in high school, and the questions will be a lot harder to answer. However, if you don't take the time to answer the questions in preschool, kindergarten, and first and second grade, your teenager may seek answers elsewhere to those very important, difficult-to-answer questions a few years from now. So start right now. Take the time. Answer every question carefully and with love.

About
the Author

Larry Cuocci

Dr. Susan Bartell is a nationally renowned psychologist and author who has been helping children, teens, and families lead healthier, happier lives for nearly twenty years. Dr. Susan has appeared on *Good Morning America*, *20/20*, and *The Today Show*, and is a frequent contributor to the *New York Times*, *Parenting* magazine, *Family Circle*, *WebMD*, *Women's Day*, *Nick Jr.*, and *Seventeen*.

3/10

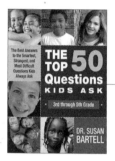